STUDIES IN OCCULTISM

COMPLETE

A Series of Reprints from the Writings

of

Helena Petrovna Blavatsky

NUMBERS

I – VI

A Yesterday's World Publishing

Published by A Yesterday's World Publishing
Copyright © 2020 A Yesterday's World Publishing
First impression 2020
ISBN - 978-1-912970-48-3

CONTENTS

STUDIES IN OCCULTISM

A Series of Reprints from the Writings

of

H. P. BLAVATSKY

NO. 1

PRACTICAL OCCULTISM

OCCULTISM VERSUS THE OCCULT ARTS

THE BLESSINGS OF PUBLICITY

Occultism is not magic, though magic is one of its tools.

Occultism is not the acquirement of powers, whether psychic or intellectual, though both are its servants. Neither is occultism the pursuit of happiness, as men understand the word; for the first step is sacrifice, the second, renunciation.

Occultism is the science of life, the art of living.—*Lucifer*, Vol. I, p. 7.

PRACTICAL OCCULTISM

AS some of the letters in the CORRESPONDENCE of this month show, there are many people who are looking for practical instruction in Occultism. It becomes necessary, therefore, to state once for all:—

(*a*) The essential difference between theoretical and practical Occultism; or what is generally known as Theosophy on the one hand, and Occult science on the other, and:—

(*b*) The nature of the difficulties involved in the study of the latter.

It is easy to become a Theosophist. Any person of average intellectual capacities, and a leaning toward the metaphysical; of pure, unselfish life, who finds more joy in helping his neighbor than in receiving help himself; one who is ever ready to sacrifice his own pleasures for the sake of other people; and who loves Truth, Goodness, and Wisdom for their own sake, not for the benefit they may confer—is a Theosophist.

But it is quite another matter to put oneself upon the path which leads to the knowledge of what is good to do, as to the right discrimination of good from evil; a path which also leads a man to that power through which he can do the good he desires, often without even apparently lifting a finger.

Moreover, there is one important fact with which the student should be made acquainted. Namely, the enormous, almost limitless responsibility assumed by the teacher for the sake of the pupil. From the Gurus of the East who teach openly or secretly, down to the few Kabalists in Western lands who undertake to teach the rudiments of the Sacred Science to their disciples—those western Hierophants being often themselves ignorant of the danger they incur—one and all of these "Teachers" are subject to the same inviolable law. From the moment they begin *really* to teach, from the instant they confer *any* power—whether psychic, mental, or physical—on their pupils, they take upon themselves *all* the sins of that pupil, in connection with the Occult Sciences, whether of omission or commission, until the moment when initiation makes the pupil a Master and responsible in his turn. There is a weird and mystic religious law, greatly reverenced and acted upon in the Greek, half-forgotten in the Roman Catholic, and absolutely extinct in the Protestant Church. It dates from the earliest days of Christianity and has its basis in the law just stated, of which it was a symbol and an expression. This is the dogma of the absolute sacredness of the relation between the god-parents who stand sponsors for a child.[1] These tacitly take upon themselves all the sins of the newly baptized child—(anointed, as at the initiation, a mystery truly!)—until the day when the child becomes a responsible unit, knowing good and evil. Thus it is clear why the "Teachers" are so reticent, and why *Chelas* are required to serve a seven years probation to prove their fitness, and develop the qualities necessary to the security of both Master and pupil.

Occultism is not magic. It is *comparatively* easy to learn the trick of spells and the methods of using the subtler, but still material, forces of physical nature; the

---

[1] So holy is the connection thus formed deemed in the Greek Church, that a marriage between god-parents of the same child is regarded as the worst kind of incest, is considered illegal, and is dissolved by law; and this absolute prohibition extends even to the children of one of the sponsors as regards those of the other.

powers of the animal soul in man are soon awakened; the forces which his love, his hate, his passion, can call into operation, are readily developed. But this is Black Magic—*Sorcery*. For it is the motive, *and the motive alone*, which makes any exercise of power become black, malignant, or white, beneficent Magic. It is impossible to employ *spiritual* forces if there is the slightest tinge of selfishness remaining in the operator. For, unless the intention is entirely unalloyed, the spiritual will transform itself into the psychic, act on the astral plane, and dire results may be produced by it. The powers and forces of animal nature can equally be used by the selfish and revengeful, as by the unselfish and the all-forgiving; the powers and forces of spirit lend themselves only to the perfectly pure in heart— and this is DIVINE MAGIC.

What are then the conditions required to become a student of the "Divina Sapientia"? For let it be known that no such instruction can possibly be given unless these certain conditions are complied with, and rigorously carried out during the years of study. This is a *sine quâ non*. No man can swim unless he enters deep water. No bird can fly unless its wings are grown, and it has space before it and courage to trust itself to the air. A man who will wield a two-edged sword, must be a thorough master of the blunt weapon, if he would not injure himself—or what is worse—others, at the first attempt.

To give an approximate idea of the conditions under which alone the study of Divine Wisdom can be pursued with safety, that is without danger that Divine will give place to Black Magic, a page is given from the "private rules," with which every instructor in the East is furnished. The few passages which follow are chosen from a great number and explained in brackets.

---

1. The place selected for receiving instruction must be a spot calculated not to distract the mind, and filled with "influence-evolving" (magnetic) objects. The five sacred colors gathered in a circle must be there among other things. The place must be free from any malignant influences hanging about in the air.

[The place must be set apart, and used for no other purpose. The five "sacred colors" are the prismatic hues arranged in a certain way, as these colors are very magnetic. By "malignant influences" are meant any disturbances through strifes, quarrels, bad feelings, etc., as these are said to impress themselves immediately on the astral light, *i.e.,* in the atmosphere of the place, and to hang "about in the air." This first condition seems easy enough to accomplish, yet—on further consideration, it is one of the most difficult ones to obtain.]

2. Before the disciple shall be permitted to study "face to face," he has to acquire preliminary understanding in a select company of other lay *upâsakas* (disciples), the number of whom must be odd.

["Face to face" means in this instance a study independent or apart from others, when the disciple gets his instruction *face to face* either with himself (his higher, Divine Self) or—his guru. It is then only that each receives *his due* of information, according to the use he has made of his knowledge. This can happen only toward the end of the cycle of instruction.]

3. Before thou (the teacher) shalt impart to thy *Lanoo* (disciple) the good (holy)

words of LAMRIN, or shalt permit him "to make ready" for *Dubjed*, thou shalt take care that his mind is thoroughly purified and at peace with all, especially *with his other Selves*. Otherwise the words of Wisdom and of the good Law, shall scatter and be picked up by the winds.

["Lamrin" is a work of practical instructions, by Tson-kha-pa, in two portions, one for ecclesiastical and exoteric purposes, the other for esoteric use. "To make ready" for *Dubjed*, is to prepare the vessels used for seership, such as mirrors and crystals. The "other selves," refers to the fellow students. Unless the greatest harmony reigns among the learners, *no* success is possible. It is the teacher who makes the selections according to the magnetic and electric natures of the students, bringing together and adjusting most carefully the positive and the negative elements.]

4. The *upâsakas* while studying must take care to be united as the fingers on one hand. Thou shalt impress upon their minds that whatever hurts one should hurt the others, and if the rejoicing of one finds no echo in the breasts of the others, then the required conditions are absent, and it is useless to proceed.

[This can hardly happen if the preliminary choice made was consistent with the magnetic requirements. It is known that *chelas* otherwise promising and fit for the reception of truth, had to wait for years on account of their temper and the impossibility they felt to put themselves *in tune* with their companions. For—]

5. The co-disciples must be tuned by the *guru* as the strings of a lute (*vina*) each different from the others, yet each emitting sounds in harmony with all. Collectively they must form a key-board answering in all its parts to thy lightest touch (the touch of the Master). Thus their minds shall open for the harmonies of Wisdom, to vibrate as knowledge through each and all, resulting in effects pleasing to the presiding gods (tutelary or patron-angels) and useful to the *Lanoo*. So shall Wisdom be impressed forever on their hearts and the harmony of the law shall never be broken.

6. Those who desire to acquire the knowledge leading to the *Siddhis* (occult powers) have to renounce all the vanities of life and of the world (here follows enumeration of the *Siddhis*).

7. None can feel the difference between himself and his fellow-students, such as "I am the wisest," "I am more holy and pleasing to the teacher, or in my community, than my brother," etc.,—and remain an *upâsaka*. His thoughts must be predominantly fixed upon his heart, chasing therefrom every hostile thought to any living being. It (the heart) must be full of the feeling of its non-separateness from the rest of beings as from all in Nature; otherwise no success can follow.

8. A *Lanoo* (disciple) has to dread external living influence alone (magnetic emanations from living creatures). For this reason while at one with all, in his *inner nature*, he must take care to separate his outer (external) body from every foreign influence: none must drink out of, or eat in his cup but himself. He must avoid bodily contact (*i.e.,* being touched or touch) with human, as with animal being.

[No pet animals are permitted, and it is forbidden even to touch certain trees and plants. A disciple has to live, so to say, in his own atmosphere in order to individualize it for occult purposes.]

9. The mind must remain blunt to all but the universal truths in nature, lest the "Doctrine of the Heart" should become only the "Doctrine of the Eye," (*i.e.*, empty exoteric ritualism).

10. No animal food of whatever kind, nothing that has life in it should be taken by the disciple. No wine, no spirits, or opium should be used; for these are like the *Lhamayin* (evil spirits), who fasten upon the unwary, they devour the understanding.

[Wine and spirits are supposed to contain and preserve the bad magnetism of all the men who helped in their fabrication; the meat of each animal, to preserve the psychic characteristics of its kind.]

11. Meditation, abstinence in all, the observation of moral duties, gentle thoughts, good deeds and kind words, as good will to all and entire oblivion of Self, are the most efficacious means of obtaining knowledge and preparing for the reception of higher wisdom.

12. It is only by virtue of a strict observance of the foregoing rules that a *Lanoo* can hope to acquire in good time the *Siddhis* of the *Arhats,* the growth which makes him become gradually One with the Universal ALL.

These 12 extracts are taken from among some 73 rules, to enumerate which would be useless as they would be meaningless in Europe. But even these few are enough to show the immensity of the difficulties which beset the path of the would-be *Upâsaka*, who has been born and bred in Western lands.[1]

All western, and especially English, education is instinct with the principle of emulation and strife; each boy is urged to learn more quickly, to outstrip his companions, and to surpass them in every possible way. What is miss-called "friendly rivalry" is assiduously cultivated, and the same spirit is fostered and strengthened in every detail of life.

With such ideas "educated into" him from his childhood, how can a Western bring himself to feel towards his co-students "as the fingers on one hand"? Those co-students, too, are not of his *own selection*, or chosen by himself from personal sympathy and appreciation. They are chosen by his teacher on far other grounds, and he who would be a student must *first* be strong enough to kill out in his heart all feelings of dislike and antipathy to others. How many Westerns are ready even to attempt this in earnest?

And then the details of daily life, the command not to touch even the hand of one's nearest and dearest. How contrary to Western notions of affection and good feeling! How cold and hard it seems. Egotistical too, people would say, to abstain from giving pleasure to others for the sake of one's own development. Well, let those who think so defer till another lifetime the attempt to enter the path in real earnest. But let them not glory in their own fancied unselfishness. For, in reality, it is only the seeming appearances which they allow to deceive them, the conventional notions, based on emotionalism and gush, or so-called courtesy,

---

[1] Be it remembered that *all Chelas,* even lay disciples, are called *Upâsaka* until after their first initiation, when they become *Lanoo-Upâsaka*. To that day, even those who belong to Lamaseries and are *set apart*, are considered as "laymen."

6

things of the unreal life, not the dictates of Truth.

But even putting aside these difficulties, which may be considered "external," though their importance is none the less great, how are students in the West to "attune themselves" to harmony as here required of them? So strong has personality grown in Europe and America, that there is no school of artists even whose members do not hate and are not jealous of each other. "Professional" hatred and envy have become proverbial; men seek each to benefit himself at all costs, and even the so-called courtesies of life are but a hollow mask covering these demons of hatred and jealousy.

In the East the spirit of "non-separateness" is inculcated as steadily from childhood up, as in the West the spirit of rivalry. Personal ambition, personal feelings and desires, are not encouraged to grow so rampant there. When the soil is naturally good, it is cultivated in the right way, and the child grows into a man in whom the habit of subordination of one's lower to one's higher Self is strong and powerful. In the West men think that their own likes and dislikes of other men and things are guiding principles for them to act upon, even when they do not make of them the law of their lives and seek to impose them upon others.

Let those who complain that they have learned little in the Theosophical Society lay to heart the words written in an article in the *Path* for last February:— "The key in each degree is the *aspirant himself*." It is not "the fear of God" which is "the beginning of Wisdom," but the knowledge of self which is wisdom itself.

How grand and true appears, thus, to the student of Occultism who has commenced to realize some of the foregoing truths, the answer given by the Delphic Oracle to all who came seeking after Occult Wisdom—words repeated and enforced again and again by the wise Socrates:—

MAN KNOW THY-SELF.

Chelaship has nothing *whatever* to do with means of subsistence or anything of

7

the kind, for a man can isolate his mind entirely from his body and its surroundings. Chelaship is a *state of mind,* rather than a life according to hard and fast rules, on the physical plane. This applies especially to the earlier, probationary period, while the rules given in *Lucifer* for April last pertain properly to a later stage, that of actual occult training and the development of occult powers and insight. These rules indicate, however, the mode of life which ought to be followed by all aspirants *so far as practicable,* since it is the most helpful to them in their aspirations.

It should never be forgotten that Occultism is concerned with the *inner man,* who must be strengthened and freed from the dominion of the physical body and its surroundings, which must become his servants. Hence the *first* and chief necessity of Chelaship is a spirit of absolute unselfishness and devotion to Truth; then follow self-knowledge and self-mastery. These are all-important; while outward observance of fixed rules of life is a matter of secondary moment.

—*Lucifer:* IV, 348, note.

OCCULTISM VERSUS THE
OCCULT ARTS

"I oft have heard, but ne'er believed till now,
There are, who can by potent magic spells
Bend to their crooked purpose Nature's laws."

—*Milton*

IN this month's Correspondence several letters testify to the strong impression produced on some minds by our last month's article "Practical Occultism." Such letters go far to prove and strengthen two logical conclusions:—

(*a*) There are more well-educated and thoughtful men who believe in the existence of Occultism and Magic (the two differing vastly) than the modern materialist dreams of; and:—

(*b*) That most of the believers (comprising many theosophists) have no definite idea of the nature of Occultism and confuse it with the Occult sciences in general, the "Black art" included.

Their representations of the powers it confers upon man, and of the means to be used to acquire them are as varied as they are fanciful. Some imagine that a master in the art, to show the way, is all that is needed to become a Zanoni. Others, that one has but to cross the Canal of Suez and go to India to bloom forth as a Roger Bacon or even a Count St. Germain. Many take for their ideal Margrave with his ever-renewing youth, and care little for the soul as the price paid for it. Not a few, mistaking "Witch-of-Endorism" pure and simple, for Occultism— "through the yawning Earth from Stygian gloom, call up the meager ghost to walks of light," and want, on the strength of this feat, to be regarded as full blown Adepts. "Ceremonial Magic" according to the rules mockingly laid down by Éliphas Lévi, is another imagined *alter ego* of the philosophy of the Arhats of old. In short, the prisms through which Occultism appears, to those innocent of the philosophy, are as multicolored and varied as human fancy can make them.

Will these candidates to Wisdom and Power feel very indignant if told the plain truth? It is not only useful, but it has now become *necessary* to disabuse most of them and before it is too late. This truth may be said in a few words: There are not in the West half-a-dozen among the fervent hundreds who call themselves "Occultists," who have even an approximately correct idea of the nature of the Science they seek to master. With a few exceptions, they are all on the highway to Sorcery. Let them restore some order in the chaos that reigns in their minds, before they protest against this statement. Let them first learn the true relation in which the Occult Sciences stand to Occultism, and the difference between the two, and then feel wrathful if they still think themselves right. Meanwhile, let them learn that Occultism differs from Magic and other secret Sciences as the glorious Sun does from a rush-light, as the immutable and immortal Spirit of Man—the reflection of the absolute, causeless, and unknowable ALL,—differs from the mortal clay—the human body.

In our highly civilized West, where modern languages have been formed, and words coined, in the wake of ideas and thoughts—as happened with every tongue—the more the latter became materialized in the cold atmosphere of Western selfishness and its incessant chase after the goods of this world, the less was there any need felt for the production of new terms to express that which was tacitly regarded as obsolete and exploded "superstition." Such words could answer only to ideas which a cultured man was scarcely supposed to harbor in his mind. "Magic," a synonym for jugglery; "Sorcery," an equivalent for crass ignorance; and "Occultism," the sorry relic of crack-brained, medieval Fire-philosophers, of the Jacob Boehmes and the St. Martins, are expressions believed more than amply sufficient to cover the whole field of "thimble-rigging." They are terms of contempt, and used generally only in reference to the dross and residues of the Dark Ages and its preceding æons of paganism. Therefore have we no terms in the English tongue to define and shade the difference between such abnormal powers, or the sciences that lead to the acquisition of them, with the nicety possible in the Eastern languages—pre-eminently the Sanskrit. What do the words "miracle" and "enchantment" (words identical in meaning after all, as both express the idea of producing wonderful things by *breaking the laws of nature* (*! !*) as explained by the accepted authorities) convey to the minds of those who hear, or who pronounce them? A Christian—*breaking* "of the laws of nature," notwithstanding—while believing firmly in the *miracles*, because said to have been produced by God through Moses, will either scout the enchantments performed by Pharoah's magicians, or attribute them to the devil. It is the latter whom our pious enemies connect with Occultism, while their impious foes, the infidels, laugh at Moses, Magicians, and Occultists, and would blush to give one serious thought to such "superstitions." This, because there is no term in existence to show the difference; no words to express the lights and shadows and draw the line of demarcation between the sublime and the true, the absurd and the ridiculous. The latter are the theological interpretations which teach the "breaking of the laws of Nature" by man, God, or devil; the former—the *scientific* "miracles" and enchantments of Moses and the Magicians *in accordance with natural laws*, both having been learned in all the Wisdom of the Sanctuaries, which were the "Royal Societies" of those days—and in true OCCULTISM. This last word is certainly misleading, translated as it stands from the compound word *Guptâ-Vidyâ*, "Secret Knowledge." But the knowledge of what? Some of the Sanskrit terms may help us.

There are four (out of the many other) names of the various kinds of Esoteric Knowledge or Sciences given, even in the exoteric *Purânas*. There is (1) *Yajña-Vidyâ*,[1] knowledge of the occult powers awakened in Nature by the performance of certain religious ceremonies and rites. (2) *Mahâ-Vidyâ*, the "great knowledge," the magic of the Kabalists and of the *Tântrika* worship, often Sorcery of the worst description. (3) *Guhyâ-Vidyâ*, knowledge of the mystic powers residing in Sound (Ether), hence in the *Mantras* (chanted prayers or incantations) and depending on the rhythm and melody used; in other words a magical performance based on

---

[1] "The *Yajña*," say the Brâhmans, "exists from eternity, for it proceeded forth from the Supreme One ... in whom it lay dormant from '*no* beginning.' It is the key to the TRAIVIDYA, the thrice sacred science contained in the *Rig* verses, which teaches the *Yagus* or sacrificial mysteries. 'The *Yajña*' exists as an invisible thing at all times; it is like the latent power of electricity in an electrifying machine, requiring only the operation of a suitable apparatus in order to be elicited. It is supposed to extend from the *Ahavaniya* or sacrificial fire to the heavens, forming a bridge or ladder by means of which the sacrificer can communicate with the world of gods and spirits, and even ascend when alive to their abodes."—Martin Haug's *Aitareya Brâhmana*.

"This *Yajña* is again one of the forms of the *Âkâśa*; and the mystic word calling it into existence and pronounced mentally by the initiated Priest is the Lost Word receiving impulse through will power."—*Isis Unveiled*, Vol. I. Introduction. See *Aitareya Brâhmana*, Hauge.

Knowledge of the Forces of Nature and their correlation; and (4) ÂTMA-VIDYÂ, a term which is translated simply "Knowledge of the Soul," *true Wisdom* by the Orientalists, but which means far more.

This last is the only kind of Occultism that any Theosophist who admires *Light on the Path*, and who would be wise and unselfish, ought to strive after. All the rest is some branch of the "Occult Sciences," *i.e.,* arts based on the knowledge of the ultimate essence of all things in the Kingdom of Nature—such as minerals, plants, and animals—hence of things pertaining to the realm of *material* Nature, however invisible that essence may be, and howsoever much it has hitherto eluded the grasp of Science. Alchemy, Astrology, Occult Physiology, Chiromancy exist in Nature, and the *exact* Sciences—perhaps so called because they are found in this age of paradoxical philosophies the reverse—have already discovered not a few of the secrets of the above *arts*. But clairvoyance, symbolized in India as the "Eye of Śiva," called in Japan, "Infinite Vision," is *not* Hypnotism, the illegitimate son of Mesmerism, and is not to be acquired by such arts. All the others may be mastered and results obtained, whether good, bad, or indifferent; but *Âtma-Vidyâ* sets small value on them. It includes them all, and may even use them occasionally, but it does so after purifying them of their dross, for beneficent purposes, and taking care to deprive them of every element of selfish motive. Let us explain: Any man or woman can set himself or herself to study one or all of the above specified "Occult Arts" without any great previous preparation, and even without adopting any too restraining mode of life. One could even dispense with any lofty standard of morality. In the last case, of course, ten to one the student would blossom into a very decent kind of sorcerer, and tumble down headlong into black magic. But what can this matter? The *Voodoos* and the *Dugpas* eat, drink and are merry over hecatombs of victims of their infernal arts. And so do the amiable gentlemen vivisectionists and the *diploma-ed* "Hypnotizers" of the Faculties of Medicine; the only difference between the two classes being that the Voodoos and the Dugpas are *conscious*, and the Charcot-Richet crew *unconscious* Sorcerers. Thus, since both have to reap the fruits of their labors and achievements in the black art, the Western practitioners should not have the punishment and reputation without the profits and enjoyments they may get there from. For we say it again, *hypnotism* and *vivisection* as practised in such schools, are *Sorcery* pure and simple, *minus* a knowledge that the Voodoos and Dugpas enjoy, and which no Charcot-Richet can procure for himself in fifty years of hard study and experimental observation. Let then those who will dabble in magic, whether they understand its nature or not, but who find the rules imposed upon students too hard, and who, therefore, lay *Âtma-Vidyâ* or Occultism aside—go without it. Let them become magicians by all means, even though they do become *Voodoos* and *Dugpas* for the next ten incarnations.

But the interest of our readers will probably center on those who are invincibly attracted towards the "Occult," yet who neither realize the true nature of what they aspire towards, nor have they become passion-proof, far less truly unselfish.

How about these unfortunates, we shall be asked, who are thus rent in twain by conflicting forces? For it has been said too often to need repetition, and the fact itself is patent to any observer, that when once the desire for Occultism has really awakened in a man's heart, there remains for him no hope of peace, no place of rest and comfort in all the world. He is driven out into the wild and desolate spaces of life by an ever-gnawing unrest he cannot quell. His heart is too full of passion and selfish desire to permit him to pass the Golden Gate; he cannot find rest or peace in ordinary life. Must he then inevitably fall into sorcery and black magic, and through many incarnations heap up for himself a terrible Karma? Is there no other road for him?

Indeed there is, we answer. Let him aspire to no higher than he feels able to accomplish. Let him not take a burden upon himself too heavy for him to carry. Without ever becoming a "Mahâtmâ," a Buddha, or a Great Saint, let him study the philosophy and the "Science of Soul," and he can become one of the modest benefactors of humanity, without any "superhuman" powers. *Siddhis* (or the Arhat powers) are only for those who are able to "lead the life," to comply with the terrible sacrifices required for such a training, and to comply with them *to the very letter*. Let them know at once and remember always, that *true Occultism or Theosophy* is the "Great Renunciation of SELF," unconditionally and absolutely, in thought as in action. It is altruism, and it throws him who practises it out of calculation of the ranks of the living altogether. "Not for himself, but for the world, he lives," as soon as he has pledged himself to the work. Much is forgiven during the first years of probation. But, no sooner is he "accepted" than his personality must disappear, and he has to become *a mere beneficent force in Nature*. There are two poles for him after that, two paths, and no midward place of rest. He has either to ascend laboriously, step by step, often through numerous incarnations and *no Devachanic break*, the golden ladder leading to Mahâtmâship (the *Arhat* or *Bodhisattva* condition), or—he will let himself slide down the ladder at the first false step, and roll down into *Dugpaship*. . . .

All this is either unknown or left out of sight altogether. Indeed, one who is able to follow the silent evolution of the preliminary aspirations of the candidates, often finds strange ideas quietly taking possession of their minds. There are those whose reasoning powers have been so distorted by foreign influences that they imagine that animal passions can be so sublimated and elevated that their fury, force, and fire can, so to speak, be turned inwards; that they can be stored and shut up in one's breast, until their energy is, not expanded, but turned toward higher and more holy purposes; namely, *until their collective and unexpanded strength enables their possessor to enter the true Sanctuary of the Soul* and stand therein in the presence of the *Master*—the HIGHER SELF! For this purpose they will not struggle with their passions nor slay them. They will simply, by a strong effort of will put down the fierce flames and keep them at bay within their natures, allowing the fire to smolder under a thin layer of ashes. They submit joyfully to the torture of the Spartan boy who allowed the fox to devour his entrails rather than part with it. Oh, poor, blind visionaries!

As well hope that a band of drunken chimney-sweeps, hot and greasy from their work, may be shut up in a Sanctuary hung with pure white linen, and that instead of soiling and turning it by their presence into a heap of dirty shreds, they will become masters in and of the sacred recess, and finally emerge from it as immaculate as that recess. Why not imagine that a dozen of skunks imprisoned in the pure atmosphere of a *Dgon-pa* (a monastery) can issue out of it impregnated with all the perfumes of the incenses used? . . . Strange aberration of the human mind. Can it be so? Let us argue.

The "Master" in the Sanctuary of our souls is "the Higher Self"—the divine spirit whose consciousness is based upon and derived solely (at any rate during the mortal life of the man in whom it is captive) from the Mind, which we have agreed to call the *Human Soul* (the "Spiritual Soul" being the vehicle of the Spirit). In its turn the former (the *personal* or human soul) is a compound in its highest form, of spiritual aspirations, volitions and divine love; and in its lower aspect, of animal desires and terrestrial passions imparted to it by its associations with its vehicle, the seat of all these. It thus stands as a link and a medium between the animal nature of man which its higher reason seeks to subdue, and his divine spiritual nature to which it gravitates, whenever it has the upper hand in its struggle with the *inner animal*. The latter is the instinctual "animal Soul" and is the hotbed of those passions, which, as just shown, are lulled instead of being killed, and locked up in their breasts by some imprudent enthusiasts. Do they still hope to turn thereby the muddy stream of the animal sewer into the crystalline waters of life? And where, on what neutral ground can they be imprisoned so as not to affect man? The fierce passions of love and lust are still alive and they are allowed to still remain in the place of their birth—*that same animal soul*; for both the higher and the lower portions of the "Human Soul" or Mind reject such inmates, though they cannot avoid being tainted with them as neighbors. The "Higher Self" or Spirit is as unable to assimilate such feelings as water to get mixed with oil or unclean liquid tallow. It is thus the mind alone—the sole link and medium between the man of earth and the Higher Self—that is the only sufferer, and which is in the incessant danger of being dragged down by those passions that may be reawakened at any moment, and perish in the abyss of matter. And how can it ever attune itself to the divine harmony of the highest Principle, when that harmony is destroyed by the mere presence, within the Sanctuary in preparation, of such animal passions? How can harmony prevail and conquer, when the soul is stained and distracted with the turmoil of passions and the terrestrial desires of the bodily senses, or even of the "Astral man"?

For this "Astral"—the shadowy "double" (in the animal as in man)—is not the companion of the *divine Ego* but of the *earthly body*. It is the link between the personal Self, the lower consciousness of *Manas* and the Body, and is the vehicle of *transitory, not of immortal life*. Like the shadow projected by man, it follows his movements and impulses slavishly and mechanically, and leans therefore to matter without ever ascending to Spirit. It is only when the power of the passions is dead altogether, and when they have been crushed and annihilated in the retort of an unflinching will; when not only all the lusts and longings of the flesh are dead, but also the recognition of the personal Self is killed out and the "astral" has been reduced in consequence to a cipher, that the Union with the "Higher Self" can take place. Then when the "astral" reflects only the conquered man, the still living, but no more the longing, selfish personality, then the brilliant *Augoeides*, the divine Self, can vibrate in conscious harmony with both the poles of the human Entity—the man of matter purified, and the ever pure Spiritual Soul—and stand in the presence of the MASTER SELF, the Christos of the mystic Gnostics, blended, merged into, and one with IT for ever.[1]

How then can it be thought possible for a man to enter the "strait gate" of occultism when his daily and hourly thoughts are bound up with worldly things, desires of possession and power, with lust, ambition and duties, which, however honorable, are still of the earth earthy? Even the love for wife and family—the purest as the most unselfish of human affections—is a barrier to *real* occultism. For whether we take as an example the holy love of a mother for her child, or that of a husband for his wife, even in these feelings, when analysed to the very bottom, and thoroughly sifted, there is still *selfishness* in the first, and an *égoisme à deux* in the second instance. What mother would not sacrifice without a moment's hesitation hundreds and thousands of lives for that of the child of her heart? and what lover or true husband would not break the happiness of every other man and woman around him to satisfy the desire of one whom he loves? This is but natural, we shall be told. Quite so; in the light of the code of human affections; less so, in that of divine universal love. For, while the heart is full of thoughts for a little group of *selves*, near and dear to us, how shall the rest of mankind fare in our souls? What percentage of love and care will there remain to bestow on the "great orphan"? And how shall the "still small voice" make itself heard in a soul entirely occupied with its own privileged tenants? What room is there left for the needs of Humanity *en bloc* to impress themselves upon, or even receive a speedy response? And yet, he who would profit by the wisdom of the universal mind, has to reach it through *the whole of Humanity* without distinction of race, complexion, religion or social status. It is *altruism*, not *egoism* even in its most legal and noble conception, that can lead the unit to merge its little Self in the Universal Selves. It is to *these* needs and to this work that the true disciple of true Occultism has to devote himself, if he would obtain *theo*sophy, divine Wisdom and Knowledge.

The aspirant has to choose absolutely between the life of the world and the life of Occultism. It is useless and vain to endeavor to unite the two, for no one can serve two masters and satisfy both. No one can serve his body and the higher Soul, and do his family duty and his universal duty, without depriving either one or the other of its rights; for he will either lend his ear to the "still small voice" and fail to hear the cries of his little ones, or, he will listen but to the wants of the latter and remain deaf to the voice of Humanity. It would be a ceaseless, a maddening struggle for almost any married man, who would pursue true practical Occultism, instead of its *theoretical* philosophy. For he would find himself ever hesitating between the voice of the impersonal divine love of Humanity, and that of the personal, terrestrial love. And this could only lead him to fail in one or the other, or perhaps in both his duties. Worse than this; for, *whoever indulges, after having pledged himself to* OCCULTISM, *in the gratification of a terrestrial love or lust,* must feel an almost immediate result; that of being irresistibly dragged from the impersonal divine state down to the lower plane of matter. Sensual, or even mental self-gratification, involves the immediate loss of the powers of spiritual

---

[1] Those who would feel inclined to see three *Egos* in one man will show themselves unable to perceive the metaphysical meaning. Man is a trinity composed of Body, Soul and Spirit; but *man* is nevertheless *one* and is surely not his body. It is the latter which is the property, the transitory clothing of the man. The three "Egos" are MAN in his three aspects on the astral, intellectual or psychic, and the Spiritual planes, or states.

discernment; the voice of the master can no longer be distinguished from that of one's passions or *even that of a Dugpa*; the right from wrong; sound morality from mere casuistry. The Dead Sea fruit assumes the most glorious mystic appearance, only to turn to ashes on the lips, and to gall in the heart, resulting in:—

"Depth ever deepening, darkness darkening still;
  Folly for wisdom, guilt for innocence;
  Anguish for rapture, and for hope despair."

And once being mistaken and having acted on their mistakes, most men shrink from realizing their error, and thus descend deeper and deeper into the mire. And, although it is the intention that decides primarily whether *white* or *black* magic is exercised, yet the results even of involuntary, unconscious sorcery cannot fail to be productive of bad Karma. Enough has been said to show that *sorcery is any kind of evil influence exercised upon other persons, who suffer, or make other persons suffer, in consequence.* Karma is a heavy stone splashed in the quiet waters of Life; and it must produce ever widening circles of ripples, carried wider and wider, almost *ad infinitum.* Such causes produced have to call forth effects, and these are evidenced in the just laws of Retribution.

Much of this may be avoided if people will only abstain from rushing into practices neither the nature nor importance of which they understand. No one is expected to carry a burden beyond his strength and powers. There are "natural-born magicians"; Mystics and Occultists by birth, and by right of direct inheritance from a series of incarnations and æons of suffering and failures. These are passion-proof, so to say. No fires of earthly origin can fan into a flame any of their senses or desires; no human voice can find response in their souls, except the great cry of Humanity. These only may be certain of success. But they can be met only far and wide, and they pass through the narrow gates of Occultism because they carry no personal luggage of human transitory sentiments along with them. They have got rid of the feeling of the lower personality, paralysed thereby the "astral" animal, and the golden, but narrow gate is thrown open before them. Not so with those who have to carry yet for several incarnations the burden of sins committed in previous lives, and even in their present existence. For such, unless they proceed with great caution, the golden gate of Wisdom may get transformed into the wide gate and the broad way "that leadeth unto destruction," and therefore "many be they that enter in thereby." This is the Gate of the Occult arts, practised for selfish motives and in the absence of the restraining and beneficent influence of ÂTMA-VIDYÂ. We are in the Kali Yuga and its fatal influence is a thousand-fold more powerful in the West than it is in the East; hence the easy preys made by the Powers of the Age of Darkness in this cyclic struggle, and the many delusions under which the world is now laboring. One of these is the relative facility with which men fancy they can get at the "Gate" and cross the threshold of Occultism without any great sacrifice. It is the dream of most Theosophists, one inspired by desire for Power and personal selfishness, and it is not such feelings that can ever lead them to the coveted goal. For, as well said by one believed to have sacrificed himself for Humanity—"Strait is the gate and narrow is the way which leadeth unto life" eternal, and therefore "few there be that find it." So strait indeed, that at the bare mention of some of the preliminary difficulties the affrighted Western candidates turn back and retreat with a shudder. . . .

15

Let them stop here and attempt no more in their great weakness. For if, while turning their backs on the narrow gate, they are dragged by their desire for the Occult one step in the direction of the broad and more inviting gates of that golden mystery which glitters in the light of illusion, woe to them! It can lead only to Dugpa-ship, and they will be sure to find themselves very soon landed on that *Via Fatale* of the *Inferno*, over whose portal Dante read the words:—

"Per me si va nella citta dolente
Per me si va nell' eterno dolore
Per me si va tra la perduta gente. . . ."

THE BLESSINGS OF PUBLICITY

A WELL-KNOWN public lecturer, a distinguished Egyptologist, said, in one of his lectures against the teachings of Theosophy, a few suggestive words, which are now quoted and must be answered:—

It is a delusion to suppose there is anything in the experience or wisdom of the past, the ascertained results of which can only be communicated from beneath the cloak and mask of mystery.... Explanation is the Soul of Science. They will tell you *we cannot have their knowledge without living their life*.... Public experimental research, the printing press, and a free-thought platform, have abolished the need of mystery. It is no longer necessary for science to take the veil, as she was forced to do for security in times past. . . .

This is a very mistaken view in one aspect. "Secrets of the purer and profounder life" not only *may* but *must* be made universally known. But *there are secrets that kill* in the arcana of Occultism, and unless a man *lives the life* he cannot be entrusted with them.

The late Professor Faraday had very serious doubts whether it was quite wise and reasonable to give out to the public at large certain discoveries of modern science. Chemistry had led to the invention of too terrible means of destruction in our century to allow it to fall into the hands of the profane. What man of sense—in the face of such fiendish applications of dynamite and other explosive substances as are made by those incarnations of the Destroying Power, who glory in calling themselves Anarchists and Socialists—would not agree with us in saying:—Far better for mankind that it should never have blasted a rock by modern perfected means, than that it should have shattered the limbs of one per cent even of those who have been thus destroyed by the pitiless hand of Russian Nihilists, Irish Fenians, and Anarchists. That such discoveries, and chiefly their murderous application, ought to have been withheld from public knowledge may be shown on the authority of statistics and commissions appointed to investigate and record the result of the evil done. The following information gathered from public papers will give an insight into what may be in store for wretched mankind.

England alone—the center of civilization—has 21,268 firms fabricating and selling explosive substances.[1] But the centers of the dynamite trade, of infernal machines, and other such results of modern civilization, are chiefly at Philadelphia and New York. It is in the former city of "Brotherly Love" that the now most famous manufacturer of explosives flourishes. It is one of the well-known respectable citizens—the inventor and manufacturer of the most murderous "dynamite toys"—who, called before the Senate of the United States anxious to adopt means for the repression of a *too free trade* in such implements, found an argument that ought to become immortalized for its cynical sophistry—"My machines," that expert is reported to have said—"are quite *harmless to look at*; as they may be manufactured in the shape of oranges, hats, boats, and anything one likes. . . . Criminal is he who murders people by means of such machines, not he

----

[1] Nitro-glycerin has found its way even into medical compounds. Physicians and druggists are vying with the Anarchists in their endeavors to destroy the surplus of mankind. The famous chocolate tablets against dyspepsia are said to contain nitro-glycerin! They may save, but they can kill still more easily.

who manufactures them. The firm refuses to admit that were there no supply there would be no incentive for demand on the market; but insists that every demand should be satisfied by a supply ready at hand."

That "supply" is the fruit of civilization and of the publicity given to the discovery of every murderous property in matter. What is it? As found in the Report of the Commission appointed to investigate the variety and character of the so-called "infernal machines," so far the following implements of instantaneous human destruction are already on hand. The most fashionable of all among the many varieties fabricated by Mr. Holgate are the "Ticker," the "Eight Day Machine," the "Little Exterminator," and the "Bottle Machines." The "Ticker" is in appearance like a piece of lead, a foot long and four inches thick. It contains an iron or steel tube full of a kind of gunpowder invented by Holgate himself. That gunpowder, in appearance like any other common stuff of that name, has, however, an explosive power two hundred times stronger than common gunpowder; the "Ticker" containing thus a powder which equals in force two hundred pounds of the common gunpowder. At one end of the machine is fastened an invisible clock-work meant to regulate the time of the explosion, which time may be fixed from one minute to thirty-six hours. The spark is produced by means of a steel needle which gives a spark at the touch-hole, and communicates thereby the fire to the whole machine.

The "Eight Day Machine" is considered the most powerful, but at the same time the most complicated, of all those invented. One must be familiar with handling it before a full success can be secured. It is owing to this difficulty that the terrible fate intended for London Bridge and its neighborhood was turned aside by the instantaneous killing instead of the two Fenian criminals. The size and appearance of that machine changes, Proteus-like, according to the necessity of smuggling it in, in one or another way, unperceived by the victims. It may be concealed in bread, in a basket of oranges, in a liquid, and so on. The Commission of Experts is said to have declared that its explosive power is such as to reduce to atoms instantly the largest edifice in the world.

The "Little Exterminator" is an innocent-looking plain utensil having the shape of a modest jug. It contains neither dynamite nor powder, but secretes, nevertheless, a deadly gas, and has a hardly perceptible clock-work attached to its edge, the needle of which points to the time when that gas will effect its escape. In a shut-up room this new "vril" of lethal kind will *smother to death, nearly instantaneously*, every living being within a distance of a hundred feet radius of the murderous jug. With these three "latest novelties" in the high season of Christian civilization, the catalog of the dynamiters is closed; all the rest belongs to the old "fashion" of the past years. It consists of hats, *porte cigars*, bottles of ordinary kind, and even *ladies' smelling bottles*, filled with dynamite, nitro-glycerin, etc., etc.—weapons, some of which, following unconsciously Karmic law, killed many of the dynamiters in the last Chicago *revolution*. Add to this the forthcoming long-promised Keeley's vibratory force, capable of reducing in a few seconds a dead bullock to a heap of ashes, and then ask yourself if the *Inferno* of Dante as a locality can ever rival earth in the production of more hellish engines of destruction?

Thus, if purely material implements are capable of blowing up, from a few corners, the greatest cities of the globe, provided the murderous weapons are guided by expert hands—what terrible dangers might not arise from magical *occult* secrets being revealed, and allowed to fall into the possession of ill-meaning persons! A thousand times more dangerous and lethal are these, because neither the criminal hand, nor the *immaterial* invisible weapon used, can ever be detected.

The congenital *black* magicians—those who, to an innate propensity towards evil, unite highly-developed mediumistic natures—are but too numerous in our age. It is nigh time then that the psychologists and believers, at least, should cease advocating the beauties of publicity and claiming knowledge of the secrets of nature for all. It is not in our age of "suggestion" and "explosives" that Occultism can open wide the doors of its laboratories except to those who *do* live the life.

H. P. B.

STUDIES IN OCCULTISM

A Series of Reprints from the Writings

of

H. P. BLAVATSKY

NO. II

HYPNOTISM

BLACK MAGIC IN SCIENCE

SIGNS OF THE TIMES

HYPNOTISM

AND ITS RELATIONS TO OTHER MODES OF FASCINATION

WE are asked by 'H. C.' and other Fellows, to answer the several queries hereafter propounded. We do so, but with a reservation: our replies must be made from the standpoint of Occultism alone, no consideration being given to such hypotheses of modern (another name for 'materialistic') Science, as may clash with esoteric teachings.

Q. *What is Hypnotism; how does it differ from Animal Magnetism (or Mesmerism)?*

ANS. Hypnotism is the new scientific name for the old ignorant 'superstition' variously called 'fascination' and 'enchantment.' It is an antiquated *lie* transformed into a modern *truth*. The fact is there, but the scientific explanation of it is still wanting. By some it is believed that *Hypnotism* is the result of an irritation artificially produced on the periphery of the nerves; that this irritation reacting upon, passes into the cells of the brain-substance, causing by exhaustion a condition which is but another mode of sleep *(hypnosis, or hupnos);* by others that it is simply a self-induced stupor, produced chiefly by imagination, etc., etc. It differs from animal magnetism where the hypnotic condition is produced by the Braid method, which is a purely mechanical one, *i.e.,* the fixing of the eyes on some bright spot, a metal or a crystal. It becomes 'animal magnetism' (or mesmerism), when it is achieved by 'mesmeric' passes on the patient, and for these reasons. When the first method is used, no electro-psychic, or even electro-physical currents are at work, but simply the mechanical, molecular vibrations of the metal or crystal gazed at by the subject. It is the *eye*—the most occult organ of all, on the superficies of our body—which, by serving as a medium between that bit of metal or crystal and the brain, *attunes* the molecular vibrations of the nervous centers of the latter into *unison (i.e.,* equality of the number of their respective oscillations) with the vibrations of the bright object held. And it is this unison which produces the hypnotic state. But in the second case, the right name for hypnotism would certainly be 'animal magnetism' or that so much derided term 'mesmerism.' For in the hypnotization by preliminary passes, it is the human will whether conscious or otherwise—of the operator himself, that acts upon the nervous system of the patient. And it is again through the vibrations—only *atomic,* not *molecular*—produced by that act of energy called WILL in the ether of space (therefore, on quite a different plane) that the *super-hypnotic state (i.e.,* 'suggestion,' etc.) is induced. For those which we call 'will-vibrations' and their aura, are absolutely distinct from the vibrations produced by the simply mechanical molecular motion, the two acting on two separate degrees of the cosmo-terrestrial planes. Here, of course, a clear realization of that which is meant by *will* in Occult Sciences, is necessary.

Q. *In both (hypnotism and animal magnetism) there is an act of will in the operator, a transit of something from him to his patient, an effect upon the patient. What is the 'something' transmitted in both cases?*

ANS. That which is transmitted has no name in European languages, and if we simply describe it as *will,* it loses all its meaning. The old and very much tabooed words, 'enchantment,' 'fascination,' 'glamor' and 'spell,' and especially the verb 'to bewitch,' expressed far more suggestively the real action that took place during the process of such a *transmission,* than the modern and meaningless terms, 'psychologize' and 'biologize.' Occultism calls the force transmitted, the 'auric *fluid,'* to distinguish it from the 'auric *light';* the 'fluid' being a correlation of *atoms* on a higher plane, and a descent to this lower one, in the shape of impalpable and invisible plastic Substances, generated and directed by the potential Will; the 'auric *light,'* or that which Reichenbach calls *Od,* a light that surrounds every animate and inanimate object in nature, is, on the other hand, but the astral reflection emanating from objects; its particular color and colors, the combinations and varieties of the latter, denoting the state of the *gunas,* or qualities and characteristics of each special object and subject— the human being's aura being the strongest of all.

Q. *What is the rationale of 'Vampirism'?*

ANS. If by this word is meant the involuntary transmission of a portion of one's vitality, or life-essence, by a kind of occult *osmosis* from one person to another— the latter being endowed, or *afflicted,* rather, with such *vampirizing* faculty, then the act can become comprehensible only when we study well the nature and essence of the semi-substantial 'auric fluid' spoken of just now. Like every other occult form in Nature, this *end-* and *exosmosic* process may be made beneficent or maleficent, either unconsciously or at will. When a healthy operator mesmerizes a patient with a determined desire to relieve and cure him, the exhaustion felt by the former is proportionate to the relief given: a process of *endosmose* has taken place, the healer having parted with a portion of his vital aura to benefit the sick man. Vampirism, on the other hand, is a blind and mechanical process, generally produced without the knowledge of either the *absorber,* or the vampirized party. It is conscious or unconscious *black* magic, as the case may be. For in the case of trained adepts and sorcerers, the process is produced consciously and with the guidance of the Will. In both cases the agent of transmission is a magnetic and attractive faculty, terrestrial and physiological in its results, yet generated and produced on the 'four-dimensional' plane—the realm of atoms.

Q. *Under what circumstances is hypnotism 'black magic'?*

ANS. Under those just discussed, but to cover the subject fully, even by giving a few instances, demands more space than we can spare for these answers. Sufficient to say that whenever the motive which actuates the operator is selfish, or detrimental to any living being or beings, all such acts are classed by us as black magic. The healthy vital fluid imparted by the physician who mesmerizes his patient, can and does cure; but too much of it will kill.

[This statement receives its explanation in our answer to Question 7, when showing that the vibratory experiment shatters a tumbler to pieces.]

Q. *Is there any difference between hypnosis produced by mechanical means, such as revolving mirrors, and that produced by the direct gaze of the operator (fascination)?*

ANS. This difference is, we believe, already pointed out in the answer to Question 1. The gaze of the operator is more potent, hence more dangerous, than the simple mechanical passes of the Hypnotizer, who in nine cases out of ten does not know how, and therefore *cannot* will. The students of Esoteric Science must be aware by the very laws of the occult correspondences that the former action is performed on the first plane of matter (the lowest), while the latter, which necessitates a well-concentrated will, has to be enacted, if the operator is a profane novice, on the *fourth,* and if he is anything of an occultist, on the *fifth plane.*

Q. *Why should a bit of crystal or a bright button throw one person into the hypnotic state and affect in no way another person? An answer to this would, we think, solve more than one perplexity.*

ANS. Science has offered several varied hypotheses upon the subject, but has not, so far, accepted any one of these as definite. This is because all such speculations revolve in the vicious circle of materio-physical phenomena with their blind forces and mechanical theories. The 'auric fluid' is *not* recognized by the men of Science, and therefore, they reject it. But have they not believed for years in the efficacy of *metallo-therapeuty,* the influence of these metals being due to the action of their electric *fluids* or currents on the nervous system? And this, simply because an analogy was found to exist between the activity of this system and electricity. The theory failed, because it clashed with the most careful observation and experiments. First of all, it was contradicted by a fundamental fact exhibited in the said metallo-therapeuty, whose characteristic peculiarity showed (a) that by no means every metal acted on every nervous disease, one patient being sensitive to some one metal, while all others produced no effect upon him; and (b) that the patients affected by certain metals were few and exceptional. This showed that 'electric fluids' operating on and curing diseases existed only in the imagination of the theorists. Had they had any actual existence, then *all* metals would affect in a greater or lesser degree, *all* patients, and every metal, taken separately, would affect every case of nervous disease, the conditions for generating such fluids being, in the given cases, precisely the same. Thus Dr. Charcot having vindicated Dr. Burke, the *once* discredited discoverer of metallo-therapeuty, Shiff and others discredited all those who believed in electric fluids, and these seem now to be given up in favor of 'molecular motion,' which now reigns supreme in physiology—*for the time being,* of course. But now arises a question: "Are the real nature, behavior and conditions of 'motion' known any better than the nature, behavior and conditions of the 'fluids'?" It is to be doubted. Anyhow, Occultism is audacious enough to maintain that electric or magnetic fluids (the two being really identical) *are due in their essence* and *origin to that same molecular motion,* now transformed into *atomic energy,*[1] to which every other phenomenon in Nature is also due. Indeed, when the needle of a galvano- or electro-meter fails to show any oscillations denoting the presence of electric or magnetic fluids, this does not prove in the least that there are none such to record; but simply that having passed on to another and higher plane of action, the electrometer can no longer be affected by the energy displayed on a plane with which it is entirely disconnected.

The above had to be explained, in order to show that the nature of the Force transmitted from one man or object to another man or object, whether in hypnotism, electricity, metallo-therapeuty or 'fascination,' is the same in essence, varying only in degree, and modified according to the sub-plane of matter it is acting on; of which sub-planes, as every occultist knows, there are seven on our

---

[1] In Occultism the word atom has a special significance, different from the one given to it by Science. See article, *Psychic and Noetic Action,* number 3 of this Series.

terrestrial plane as there are on every other.

Q. *Is Science entirely wrong in its definition of the hypnotic phenomena!*

ANS. It has no definition, so far. Now if there is one thing upon which Occultism agrees (to a certain degree) with the latest discoveries of physical Science, it is that all the bodies endowed with the property of inducing and calling forth metallo-therapeutic and other analogous phenomena, have, their great variety, notwithstanding, one feature in common. They are all the fountain heads and the generators of rapid molecular oscillations, which, whether through transmitting agents or direct contact, communicate themselves to the nervous system, changing thereby the rhythm of nervous vibrations—on the sole condition, however, of being what is called, in *unison.* Now 'unison' does not always imply the sameness of nature, or of essence, but simply the sameness of degree, a similarity with regard to gravity and acuteness, and equal potentialities for intensity of sound or motion: a bell may be in unison with a violin, and a flute with an animal or a human organ. Moreover, the rate of the number of vibrations—especially in an organic animal cell or organ, changes in accordance with the state of health and general condition. Hence the cerebral nervous centers of a hypnotic subject, while in perfect *unison,* in potential degree and essential original activity, with the object he gazes at, may yet, owing to some organic disturbance, be at the given moment at loggerheads with it, in respect to the number of their respective vibrations. In such case no hypnotic condition ensues; or no unison at all may exist between his nervous cells and the cells of the crystal or metal he is made to gaze at, in which case that particular object can never have any effect upon him. This amounts to saying that to ensure success in a hypnotic experiment, two conditions are requisite; (a) as every organic or 'inorganic' body in nature is distinguished by its fixed molecular oscillations, it is necessary to find out which are those bodies which *will* act in unison with one or another human nervous system; and (b) to remember that the molecular oscillations of the former can influence the nervous action of the latter, only when the rhythms of their respective vibrations coincide, *i.e.,* when the number of their oscillations is made identical; which, in the case of hypnotism induced by mechanical means, is achieved through the medium of the eye.

Therefore, though the difference between hypnosis produced by mechanical means, and that induced by the direct gaze of the operator, *plus* his will, depends on the plane on which the same phenomenon is produced, still the 'fascinating' or subduing agent is created by the same force at work. In the physical world and its material planes, it is called MOTION; in the worlds of mentality and metaphysics it is known as WILL—the many-faced magician throughout all nature.

As the rate of vibrations (molecular motion) in metals, woods, crystals, etc., alters under the effect of heat, cold, etc., so do the cerebral molecules change their rate, in the same way: i. e., their rate is raised or lowered. And this is what really takes place in the phenomenon of hypnotism. In the case of gazing, it is the eye— the chief agent of the Will of the active operator, but a slave and traitor when this Will is dormant—that, unconsciously to the patient or *subject,* attunes the oscillations of his cerebral nervous centers to the rate of the vibrations of the object gazed at by catching the rhythm of the latter and passing it on to the brain. But in the case of direct passes, it is the Will of the operator radiating through his eye that produces the required unison between his will and the will of the person operated upon. For, out of two objects attuned in unison as two chords, for instance—one will always be weaker than the other, and thus have mastery over the other and even the potentiality of destroying its weaker 'co-respondent.' So true is this, that we can call upon physical Science to corroborate this fact. Take the 'sensitive flame' as a case in hand. Science tells us that if a note be struck in unison with the ratio of the vibrations of the heat molecules, the flames will respond immediately to the sound (or note struck), that it will dance and sing in rhythm with the sounds. But Occult Science adds, that the flame may *also be extinguished* if the sound is intensified *(vide Isis Unveiled,* Vol. II, pp. 606 and 607). Another proof. Take a wine-glass or tumbler of very fine and clear glass; produce, by striking it gently with a silver spoon, a well-determined note; after which reproduce the same note by rubbing its rim with a damp finger, and, if you are successful, the glass will immediately crack and be shattered. Indifferent to every other sound, the glass will not resist the great intensity of its own fundamental note, for that particular vibration will cause such a commotion in its particles, that the whole fabric will fall in pieces.

Q. *What becomes of diseases cured by hypnotism; are they really cured or are they postponed, or do they appear in another form? Are diseases Karma; and, if so, is it right to attempt to cure them?*

ANS. Hypnotic suggestion may cure for ever, and it may not. All depends on the degree of magnetic relations between the operator and the patient. *If* Karmic, they will be only postponed, and return in some other form, not necessarily of disease, but as a punitive evil of another sort. It is always 'right' to try to alleviate suffering whenever we can, and to do our best for it. Because a man suffers justly imprisonment, and catches cold in his damp cell, is it a reason why the prison-doctor should not try to cure him of it?

Q. *Is it necessary that the hypnotic 'suggestions' of the operator should be spoken! Is it not enough for him to think them, and may not even HE be ignorant or unconscious of the bent he is impressing on his subject!*

ANS. Certainly not, if the *rapport* between the two is once for all firmly established. Thought is more powerful than speech in cases of a real subjugation of the will of the patient to that of his operator. But, on the other hand, unless the 'suggestion' made is for the good only of the subject, and entirely free from any selfish motive, a suggestion *by thought is an* act of *black magic* still more pregnant with evil consequences than a *spoken* suggestion. It is always wrong and unlawful to deprive a man of his free-will, *unless for his own and Society's good;* and even the former has to be done with great discrimination. Occultism regards all such promiscuous attempts as black magic and sorcery, whether conscious or otherwise.

Q. *Do the motive and character of the operator affect the result, immediate or remote?*

ANS. In so far as the hypnotizing process becomes under his operation either white or black magic, as the last answer shows.

Q. *Is it* wise *to hypnotize* a *patient not only out of a disease, but out of* a *habit such as drinking or lying?*

ANS. It is an act of charity and kindness, and this is next to wisdom. For, although the dropping of his vicious habits will add nothing to his good Karma (which it would, had his efforts to reform been personal, of his own free-will, and necessitating a great mental and physical struggle), still a successful 'suggestion'

25

prevents him from generating more bad Karma, and adding constantly to the previous record of his transgressions.

Q. *What is it that a faith-healer, when successful, practises upon himself; what tricks is he playing with his principles and with his Karma?*

ANS. Imagination is a potent help in every event of our lives. Imagination acts on Faith, and both are the draughtsmen who prepare the sketches for *Will* to engrave, more or less deeply, on the rocks of obstacles and opposition with which the path of life is strewn. Says Paracelsus: *'Faith* must confirm the imagination, for faith establishes the will. . . . Determined will is the beginning of all magical operations. . . . It is because men do not perfectly imagine and believe the result, that the arts (of magic) are uncertain, while they might be perfectly certain.' This is all the secret. Half, if not two-thirds of our ailings and diseases are the fruit of our imagination and fears. Destroy the latter and give another bent to the former, and nature will do the rest. There is nothing sinful or injurious in the methods *per se.* They turn to harm only when belief in his power becomes too arrogant and marked in the faith-healer, and when he thinks he can *will* away such diseases as need, if they are not to be fatal, the immediate help of expert surgeons and physicians.

H. P. B.

BLACK MAGIC IN SCIENCE

". . . . Commence research where modern conjecture closes its faithless wings."
(Bulwer's *Zanoni*.)

"The flat denial of yesterday has become the scientific axiom of today." (Common *Sense Aphorisms*.)

THOUSANDS of years ago the Phrygian Dactyls, the initiated priests, spoken of as the 'magicians and exorcists of sickness,' healed diseases by magnetic processes. It was claimed that they had obtained these curative powers from the powerful breath of Cybele, the many-breasted goddess, the daughter of Coelus and Terra. Indeed, her genealogy and the myths attached to it show Cybele as the personification and type of the vital essence, whose source was located by the ancients between the Earth and the starry sky, and who was regarded as the very *fons vitæ* of all that lives and breathes. The mountain air being placed nearer to that fount fortifies health and prolongs man's existence; hence, Cybele's life, as an infant, is shown in her myth as having been preserved on a mountain. This was before that *Magna* and *Bona Dea,* the prolific *Mater,* became transformed into Ceres-Demeter, the patroness of the Eleusinian Mysteries.

Animal magnetism (now called Suggestion and Hypnotism) was the principal agent in theurgic mysteries as also in the *Asclepieia*—the healing temples of Æsculapius, where the patients once admitted were treated, during the process of 'incubation,' magnetically, during their sleep.

This creative and life-giving. Force—denied and laughed at when named theurgic magic; accused for the last century as being principally based on superstition and fraud, whenever referred to as mesmerism—is now called Hypnotism, Charcotism, Suggestion, 'psychology,' and what not. But whatever the expression chosen, it will ever be a loose one if used without a proper qualification. For when epitomized with all its collateral sciences—which are all sciences within *the* science—it will be found to contain possibilities, the nature of which has never been even dreamt of by the oldest and most learned professors of the orthodox physical science. The latter, 'authorities' so-called, are no better, indeed, than innocent bald infants, when brought face to face with the mysteries of antediluvian 'mesmerism.' As stated repeatedly before, the blossoms of magic, whether white or black, divine or infernal, spring all from one root. The 'breath of Cybele'—*Âkâśa tattva,* in India—is the one chief agent, and it underlay the so-called 'miracles' and 'supernatural' phenomena in all ages, as in every clime. As the parent-root or essence is universal, so are its effects innumerable. Even the greatest adepts can hardly say where its possibilities must stop.

The key to the very alphabet of these theurgic powers was lost after the last gnostic had been hunted to death by the ferocious persecution of the Church; and as gradually Mysteries, Hierophants, Theophany and Theurgy became obliterated from the minds of men until they remained in them only as a vague tradition, all this was finally forgotten. But at the period of the Renaissance, in Germany, a learned Theosophist, a Philosopher *per ignem,* as they called themselves, rediscovered some of the lost secrets of the Phrygian priests and of the *Asclepieia.* It was the great and unfortunate physician-Occultist, Paracelsus, the greatest Alchemist of the age. That genius it was, who during the Middle Ages was the first to publicly recommend the action of the magnet in the cure of certain diseases. Theophrastus Paracelsus—the 'quack' and 'drunken impostor' in the opinion of the said scientific 'bald infants' of his day, and of their successors in ours—inaugurated among other things in the seventeenth century, that which has become a profitable branch in trade in the nineteenth. It is he who invented and used for the cure of various muscular and nervous diseases magnetized bracelets, armlets, belts, rings, collars and leglets; only his magnets cured far more efficaciously than do the electric belts of today. Van Helmont, the successor of Paracelsus, and Robert Fludd, the Alchemist and Rosicrucian, also applied magnets in the treatment of their patients. Mesmer in the eighteenth, and the Marquis de Puységur in the nineteenth century only followed in their footsteps.

In the large curative establishment founded by Mesmer at Vienna, he employed, besides magnetism, electricity, metals and a variety of woods. His fundamental doctrine was that of the Alchemists. He believed that metals, as also woods and plants have all an affinity with, and bear a close relation to the human organism. Everything in the Universe has developed from one homogeneous primordial substance differentiated into incalculable species of matter, and everything is destined to return thereinto. The secret of healing, he maintained, lies in the knowledge of correspondences and affinities between kindred atoms. Find that metal, wood, stone, or plant that has the most correspondential affinity with the body of the sufferer; and, whether through internal or external use, that particular agent imparting to the patient additional strength to fight disease—(developed generally through the introduction of some foreign element into the constitution)—and to expel it, will lead invariably to his cure. Many and marvelous were such cures effected by Anton Mesmer. Subjects with heart-disease were made well. A lady of high station, condemned to death, was completely restored to health by the application of certain sympathetic woods. Mesmer himself, suffering from acute rheumatism, cured it completely by using specially prepared magnets.

In 1774 he too happened to come across the theurgic secret of direct vital transmission; and so highly interested was he, that he abandoned all his old methods to devote himself entirely to the new discovery. Henceforward he *mesmerized* by gaze and passes, the natural magnets being abandoned. The mysterious effects of such manipulations were called by him—*animal* magnetism. This brought to Mesmer a mass of followers and disciples. The *new* force was experimented with in almost every city and town of Europe and found everywhere an actual fact.

About 1780, Mesmer settled in Paris, and soon the whole metropolis, from the Royal family down to the last hysterical *bourgeoise,* were at his feet. The clergy got frightened and cried—'the Devil'! The licensed 'leeches' felt an ever-growing deficit in their pockets; and the aristocracy and the Court found themselves on the verge of madness from mere excitement. No use repeating too well-known facts, but the memory of the reader may be refreshed with a few details he may have forgotten.

It so happened that just about that time the official Academical Science felt very proud. After centuries of mental stagnation in the realm of medicine and general ignorance, several determined steps in the direction of real knowledge had finally been made. Natural sciences had achieved a decided success, and chemistry and physics were on a fair way to progress. As the *Savants* of a century ago had not yet grown to that height of sublime modesty which characterizes so preeminently their modern successors—they felt very much puffed up with their greatness. The moment for praiseworthy humility, followed by a confession of the relative insignificance of the knowledge of the period—and even of modern knowledge for the matter of that—compared to that which the ancients knew, had not yet arrived. Those were days of naïve boasting, of the peacocks of science displaying in a body their tails, and demanding universal recognition and admiration. The Sir Oracles were not as numerous as they are now, yet their number was considerable. And indeed, had not the Dulcamaras of public fairs been just visited with ostracism? Had not the *leeches* well nigh disappeared to make room for diploma-ed physicians with royal licenses to kill and bury *a piacere, ad libitum?* Hence, the nodding 'Immortal' in his academical chair was regarded as the sole competent authority in the decision of questions he had never studied, and for rendering verdicts about that which he had never heard of. It was the REIGN OF REASON, and of Science—in its teens; the beginning of the great deadly struggle between Theology and Facts, Spirituality and Materialism. In the educated classes of Society too much faith had been succeeded by no faith at all. The cycle of Science-worship had just set in, with its pilgrimages to the Academy, the Olympus where the 'Forty Immortals' are enshrined, and its raids upon every one who refused to manifest a noisy admiration, a kind of juvenile calf's enthusiasm, at the door of the Fane of Science. When Mesmer arrived, Paris divided its allegiance between the Church, which attributed all kinds of phenomena except its own *divine miracles* to the Devil, and the Academy, which believed in neither God nor Devil, but only in its own infallible wisdom.

But there were minds which would not be satisfied with either of these beliefs. Therefore, after Mesmer had forced all Paris to crowd to his halls, waiting hours to obtain a place in a chair round the miraculous *baguet,* some people thought that it was time real truth should be found out. They laid their legitimate desires at the royal feet, and the King forthwith commanded his learned Academy to look into the matter. Then it was, that awakening from their chronic nap, the 'Immortals' appointed a committee of investigation, among whom was Benjamin Franklin, and chose some of the oldest, wisest, and baldest among their 'Infants' to watch over the committee. This was in 1784. Every one knows what was the report of the latter and the final decision of the Academy. The whole transaction looks now like a general rehearsal of the play, one of the acts of which was performed by the 'Dialectical Society' of London and some of England's greatest Scientists, some eighty years later.

Indeed, notwithstanding a counter report by Dr. Jussieu, an Academician of the highest rank, and the Court physician D'Eslon, who, as eye-witnesses to the most striking phenomena, demanded that a careful investigation should be made by the Medical Faculty of the therapeutic effects of the magnetic fluid—their demand fell through. The Academy disbelieved her most eminent Scientists. Even Sir B. Franklin, so much at home with cosmic electricity, would not recognize its fountain head and primordial source, and along with Bailly, Lavoisier, Magendie, and others, proclaimed Mesmerism a delusion. Nor had the second investigation which followed the first—namely in 1825—any better results. The report was once more squashed *(vide Isis Unveiled,* Vol. I, pp. 171-176).

Even now when experiment has amply demonstrated that 'Mesmerism' or Animal Magnetism, now known as Hypnotism (a sorry effect, forsooth, of the

'Breath of Cybele') is a *fact, we* yet get the majority of scientists denying its actual existence. Small fry as it is in the majestic array of experimental psycho-magnetic phenomena, even hypnotism seems too incredible, *too mysterious,* for our Darwinists and Hæckelians. One needs too much moral courage, you see, to face the suspicion of one's colleagues, the doubt of the public, and the giggling of fools. "Mystery and charlatanism go hand in hand," they say; and "self-respect and the dignity of the profession," as Magendie remarks in his *Physiologie Humaine,* "demand that the well-informed physician should remember how readily mystery glides into charlatanism." Pity the 'well informed physician' should fail to remember that Physiology among the rest is full of mystery—profound, inexplicable mystery from A to Z—and ask whether, starting from the above 'truism,' he should not throw overboard Biology and Physiology as the greatest pieces of charlatanry in modern Science. Nevertheless, a few of the well-meaning minority of our physicians have taken up seriously the investigation of hypnotism. But even they, having been reluctantly compelled to confess the reality of its phenomena, still persist in seeing in such manifestations no higher a factor at work than the purely material and physical forces, and deny these their legitimate name of animal magnetism. But as the Rev. Mr. Haweis (of whom more presently) just said in the *Daily Graphic* . . . "The Charcot phenomena are, for all that, in many ways identical with the mesmeric phenomena, and Hypnotism must properly be considered rather as a branch of mesmerism than as something distinct from it. Anyhow, Mesmer's facts, now generally accepted, were at first stoutly denied." And they are still so denied.

But while they deny Mesmerism, they rush into Hypnotism, despite the now scientifically recognized dangers of this science, in which medical practitioners in France are, far ahead of the English. And what the former say is, that between the two states of mesmerism (or magnetism as they call it, across the water) and hypnotism "there is an abyss." The one is beneficent, the other maleficent, as it evidently must be; since, according to both Occultism and modern Psychology, *hypnotism is produced by the withdrawal of the nervous fluid from the capillary nerves,* which being, so to say the sentries that keep the doors of our senses opened, getting *anaesthetized* under hypnotic conditions, allow these to get closed. A. H. Simonin reveals many a wholesome truth in his excellent work, *Solution du Probleme de la suggestion hypnotique.*[1] Thus he shows that while "in Magnetism (mesmerism) there occurs in the *subject* a great development of moral faculties"; that his thoughts and feelings "become loftier, and the senses acquire an abnormal acuteness"; in hypnotism, on the contrary, "the subject becomes a *simple* mirror." It is Suggestion which is the true motor of every action in the hypnotic: and if, occasionally, "seemingly marvelous actions are produced, these are due to the hypnotizer, not to the subject." Again . . . "In hypnotism instinct, *i.e.,* the *animal,* reaches its greatest development; so much so indeed, that the aphorism 'extremes meet' can never receive a better application than to magnetism and hypnotism.' How true these words, also, as to the difference between the mesmerized and the hypnotized subjects. 'In one, his ideal nature, his moral self—the reflection of his divine nature—are carried to their extreme limits, and the subject becomes almost

[1] See the review of his work in the *Journal du Magnetisme, Mai, Juin,* 1890, founded in 1845 by Baron du Potet, and now edited by H. Durville, in Paris.

a celestial being *(un ange)*. In the other, it is his *instincts* which develop in a most surprising fashion. The hypnotic lowers himself to the level of the animal. From a physiological standpoint, magnetism ('Mesmerism') is comforting and curative, and hypnotism, which is but the result of an unbalanced state, is most dangerous."

Thus the adverse Report drawn by Bailly at the end of last century has had dire effects in the present, but it had its *Karma* also. Intended to kill the 'Mesmeric' *craze,* it reacted as a death-blow to the public confidence in scientific decrees. In our day the *Non-Possumus* of the Royal Colleges and Academies is quoted on the Stock Exchange of the world's opinion at a price almost as low as the *Non-Possumus* of the Vatican. The days of authority, whether human or divine, are fast gliding away; and we see already gleaming on future horizons but one tribunal, supreme and final, before which mankind will bow—the Tribunal of Fact and Truth.

Aye, to this tribunal without appeal even liberal clergymen and famous preachers make obeisance in our day. The parts have now changed hands, and in many instances it is the successors of those who fought tooth and nail for the reality of the Devil and his direct interference with psychic phenomena, for long centuries, who come out publicly to upbraid science. A remarkable instance of this is found in an excellent letter (just mentioned) by the Rev. Mr. Haweis to the *Graphic.* The learned preacher seems to share our indignation at the unfairness of the modern scientists, at their suppression of truth, and ingratitude to their ancient teachers. His letter is so interesting that its best points must be immortalized in our magazine. Here are some fragments of it. Thus he asks:—

Why can't our scientific men say: 'We have blundered about Mesmerism; it's practically true'? Not because they are men of science, but simply because they are human. No doubt it is humiliating, when you have dogmatized in the name of science, to say, 'I was wrong.' But is it not more humiliating to be found out; and is it not most humiliating, after shuffling and wriggling hopelessly in the inexorable meshes of serried facts, to collapse suddenly, and call the hated net a 'suitable enclosure,' in which, forsooth, you don't mind being caught? Now thus, it seems to me, is precisely what Messrs. Charcot and the French hypnotists and their medical admirers in England are doing. Ever since Mesmer's death at the age of eighty, in 1815, the French and English 'Faculty,' with some honorable exceptions, have ridiculed and denied the facts as well as the theories of Mesmer, but now, in 1890, a host of scientists suddenly agree, while wiping out as best they may the name of Mesmer, to rob him of all his phenomena, which they quietly appropriate under the name of ' hypnotism,' 'suggestion,' 'Therapeutic Magnetism,' 'Psychopathic Massage,' and all the rest of it. Well, 'What's in a name?'

I care more for things than names, but I reverence the pioneers of thought who have been cast out, trodden under foot, and crucified by the orthodox of all ages, and I think the least scientists can do for men like Mesmer, Du Potet, Puységur, or Mayo and Elliotson, now they are gone, is to 'build their sepulchers.'

But Mr. Haweis might have added instead, the amateur Hypnotists of Science dig with their own hands the graves of many a man's and woman's intellect; they enslave and paralyse free-will in their 'subjects,' turn immortal men into soulless, irresponsible automata, and vivisect *their souls* with as much unconcern as they vivisect the bodies of rabbits and dogs. In short, they are fast blooming into 'sorcerers,' and are turning science into a vast field of black magic. The reverend writer, however, lets the culprits off easily: and, remarking that he accepts 'the distinction' (between Mesmerism and Hypnotism) 'without pledging himself to any theory,' he adds:—

I am mainly concerned with the facts, and what I want to know is why these cures and abnormal states are trumpeted about as modern discoveries, while the 'faculty' still deride or ignore their great predecessors without having themselves a theory which they can agree upon or a single fact which can be called new. The truth is, we are just blundering back with toil to work over again the old disused mines of the ancients; the rediscovery of these occult sciences is exactly matched by the slow recovery of sculpture and painting in modern Europe. Here is the history of occult science in a nutshell. (1) Once known. (2) Lost. (3) Rediscovered. (4) Denied. (5) Reaffirmed, and by slow degrees, under new names, victorious. The evidence for all this is exhaustive and abundant. Here it may suffice to notice that Diodorus Siculus mentions how the Egyptian priests, ages before Christ, attributed clairvoyance, induced for therapeutic purposes, to Isis. Strabo ascribes the same to Serapis, while Galen mentions a temple near Memphis famous for these Hypnotic cures. Pythagoras, who won the confidence of the Egyptian priests, is full of it. Aristophanes in 'Plutus' describes in some detail a Mesmeric cure—καὶ πρῶτα μεν δὴ τῆς κεφαλῆς ἐφήψατο, etc., 'and first he began to handle the head.' Caelius Aurelianus describes manipulations (1569) for disease 'conducting the hands from the superior to the inferior parts'; and there was an old Latin proverb—Ubi dolor ibi digitus, 'Where pain, there finger.' But time would fail me to tell of Paracelsus (1462)[1] and his 'deep secret of Magnetism'; of Van Helmont (1644)[2] and his 'faith in the power of the hand in disease.' Much in the writings of both these men was only made clear to the moderns by the experiments of Mesmer, and in view of modern Hypnotists it is clearly with him and his disciples that we have chiefly to do. He claimed, no doubt, to transmit an animal magnetic fluid, which I believe the Hypnotists deny.

They do, they do. But so did the scientists with regard to more than one truth. To deny "an animal magnetic fluid" is surely no more absurd than to deny the circulation of the blood, as they have so energetically done.

A few additional details about Mesmerism given by Mr. Haweis may prove interesting. Thus he reminds us of the answer written by the much wronged Mesmer to the Academicians after their unfavorable Report, and refers to it as 'prophetic words.'

"You say that Mesmer will never hold up his head again. If such is the destiny of the man it is not the destiny of the truth, which is in its nature imperishable, and will shine forth sooner or later in the same or some other country with more brilliancy than ever, and its triumph will annihilate its miserable detractors." Mesmer left Paris in disgust, and retired to Switzerland to die; but the illustrious Dr. Jussieu became a convert. Lavater carried Mesmer's system to Germany, while Puységur and Deleuze spread it throughout provincial France, forming innumerable 'harmonic societies' devoted to the study of therapeutic magnetism and its allied phenomena of thought-transference, hypnotism, and clairvoyance.

Some twenty years ago I became acquainted with perhaps the most illustrious disciple of Mesmer, the aged Baron du Potet.[3] Round this man's therapeutic and mesmeric exploits raged, between 1830 and 1846, a bitter controversy throughout France. A murderer had been tracked, convicted, and executed solely on evidence supplied by one of Du Potet's

[1] This date is an error. Paracelsus was born at Zurich in 1493.
[2] This is the date of Van Helmont's death; he was born in 1577.
[3] Baron du Potet was for years Honorary Member of the Theosophical Society. Autograph letters were received from him and preserved at our Headquarters, in which he deplores the flippant unscientific way in which Mesmerism (then on the eve of becoming the "hypnotism" of science) was handled "par les charlatans du jour." Had he lived to see the sacred science in its full travesty as hypnotism, his powerful voice might have stopped its terrible present abuses and degradation into a commercial Punch and Judy show. Luckily for him, and unlucky for truth, the greatest adept of Mesmerism in Europe of this century—is dead.

clairvoyantes. The *Juge de Paix* admitted thus much in open court. This was too much for even sceptical Paris, and the Academy determined to sit again and, if possible, crush out the superstition. They sat, but, strange to say, this time they were converted. Itard, Fouquier, Guersent, Bourdois *de* la Motte, the cream of the French faculty, pronounced the phenomena of mesmerism to be genuine—cures, trances, clairvoyance, thought-transference, even reading from closed books; and from that time an elaborate nomenclature was invented, blotting out as far as possible the detested names of the indefatigable men who had compelled the scientific assent, while enrolling the main facts vouched for by Mesmer, Du Potet, and Puységur among the undoubted phenomena to be accepted, on whatever theory, by medical science. . . .

Then comes the turn of this foggy island and its befogged scientists.

Meanwhile, (goes on the writer) England was more stubborn. In 1846 the celebrated Dr. Elliotson, a popular practitioner with a *vast clientèle,* pronounced the famous Harveian oration, in which he confessed his belief in Mesmerism. He was denounced by the doctors with such thorough results that he lost his practice, and died well-nigh ruined, if not heart-broken. The Mesmeric Hospital in Marylebone Road had been established by him. Operations were successfully performed under Mesmerism, and all the phenomena which have lately occurred at Leeds and elsewhere, to the satisfaction of the doctors, were produced in Marylebone fifty-six years ago. Thirty-five years ago Professor Lister did the same—but the introduction of chloroform, it being more speedy and certain as an anæsthetic, killed for a time the mesmeric treatment. The public interest in Mesmerism died down, and the Mesmeric Hospital in the Marylebone Road, which had been under a cloud since the suppression of Elliotson, was at last closed. Lately we know what has been the fate of Mesmer and Mesmerism. Mesmer is spoken of in the same breath with Count Cagliostro, and Mesmerism itself is seldom mentioned at all; but, then, we hear plenty of electro-biology, therapeutic magnetism, and hypnotism. Just so. Oh, shades of Mesmer, Puységur, Du Potet, Elliotson—*sic vos non vobis!* Still, I say, *Palmam qui meruit ferat.* When I knew Baron du Potet he was on the brink of the grave, and nearly eighty years old. He was an ardent admirer of Mesmer; he had devoted his whole life to therapeutic magnetism, and he was absolutely dogmatic on the point that a real magnetic aura passed from the mesmerist to the patient. "I will show you this," he said one day, as we both stood by the bedside of a patient in so deep a trance that we ran needles into her hands and arms without exciting the least sign or movement. The old Baron continued: "I will, at the distance of a foot or two, determine slight convulsions in any part of her body by simply moving my hand above the part, without any contact." He began at the shoulder, which soon set up a twitching. Quiet being restored, he tried the elbow, then the wrist, then the knee, the convulsions increasing in intensity according to the time employed. "Are you quite satisfied?" I said, "quite satisfied." "And," continued he, "any patient that I have tested I will undertake to operate upon through a brick wall at a time and place where the patient shall be ignorant of my presence or my purpose. This," added Du Potet, "was one of the experiences which most puzzled the Academicians at Paris. I repeated the experiment again and again under every test and condition, with almost invariable success, until the most sceptical was forced to give in."

We have accused science of gliding full sail down to the Maelstrom of Black Magic, by practising that which ancient Psychology—the most important branch of the Occult Sciences—has always declared as Sorcery in its application to the *inner* man. We are prepared to maintain what we say. We mean to prove it one of these days, in some future articles, basing ourselves on facts published and the actions produced by the Hypnotism of Vivisectionists themselves. That they are unconscious sorcerers does not make away with the fact that they do practise the Black Art *bel et bien*. In short the situation is this. The minority of the learned physicians and other scientists experiment in 'hypnotism' because they have come to see something in it; while the majority of the members of the R. C. P's still deny the actuality of animal magnetism in its mesmeric form, even under its modern mask—hypnotism. The former—entirely ignorant of the fundamental laws of animal magnetism—experiment at haphazard, almost blindly. To remain consistent with their declarations (a) that hypnotism is not mesmerism, and (b) that a magnetic aura or fluid passing from the mesmerizer (or hypnotizer) is pure fallacy—they have no right, of course, to apply the laws of the older to the younger science. Hence they interfere with, and awaken to action the most dangerous forces of nature, without being aware of it. Instead of healing diseases—the only use to which animal magnetism under its new name can be *legitimately* applied—they often inoculate the *subjects* with their own physical as well as mental ills and vices. For this, and the ignorance of their colleagues of the minority, the disbelieving majority of the Sadducees are greatly responsible. For, by opposing them, they impede free action, and take advantage of the Hypocratic oath, to make them powerless to admit and do much that the believers might and would otherwise do. But as Dr. A. Teste truly says in his work—"*There are certain unfortunate truths which compromise those who believe in them, and those especially who are so candid as to avow them publicly.*" Thus the reason of hypnotism not being studied on its proper lines is self-evident.

Years ago it was remarked: 'It is the duty of the Academy and medical authorities to study Mesmerism (*i.e.*, the occult sciences in its spirit) and to subject it to trials; finally, *to take away the use and practice of it from persons quite strangers to the art, who abuse this means, and make it an object of lucre and speculation.*' He who uttered this great truth was 'the voice speaking in the desert.' But those having some experience in occult psychology would go further. They would say it is incumbent on every scientific body—nay, on every government— to put an end to public exhibitions of this sort. By trying the *magic* effect of the human will on weaker wills; by deriding the existence of *occult* forces in Nature— forces whose name is legion—and yet calling out these, under the pretext that they are *no* independent forces at all, not even psychic in their nature, but "connected with known *physical* laws," (Binet and Féré), men in authority are virtually responsible for all the dire effects that are and will be following their dangerous public experiments. Verily Karma—the terrible but just Retributive Law—will visit all those who develop the most awful results in the future, generated at those public exhibitions for the amusement of the profane. Let them only think of dangers bred, of new forms of diseases, mental and physical, begotten by such insane handling of psychic will! This is as bad on the moral plane as the artificial introduction of animal matter into the human blood, by the infamous Brown-Sequard method, is on the physical. They laugh at the occult sciences and deride Mesmerism. Yet this century will not have passed away before they have undeniable proofs that the idea of a crime suggested for experiment's sake is not removed by a reversed current of the will as easily as it is inspired. They may learn that if the outward expression of the idea of a misdeed 'suggested' may fade out at the will of the operator, the *active living germ* artificially implanted does not disappear with it; that once dropped into the seat of the human—or, rather, the animal—passions, it may lie dormant there for years sometimes, to become suddenly awakened by some unforeseen circumstances into realization. Crying children frightened into silence by the *suggestion* of a monster, a devil standing in the corner, by a foolish nurse, have been known to become insane twenty or thirty years later on the same subject. There are mysterious, secret drawers, dark nooks and hiding-places in the labyrinth of our memory, still unknown to physiologists, and which open only once, rarely twice, in man's life-time, and that only under very abnormal and peculiar conditions. But when they do, it is always some heroic deed committed by a person the least calculated for it, or—a terrible crime perpetrated, the reason for which remains forever a mystery. . .

Thus experiments in 'suggestion' by persons ignorant of the occult laws, are the most dangerous of pastimes. The action and reaction of ideas on the *inner lower* 'Ego,' has never been studied so far, because that Ego itself is *terra incognita* (even when not denied) to the men of science. Moreover, such performances before a promiscuous public are a danger in themselves. Men of undeniable scientific education who experiment on Hypnotism in public, lend thereby the sanction of their names to such performances.

And then every unworthy speculator acute enough to understand the process may, by developing by practice and perseverance the same force in himself, apply it to his own selfish, often criminal ends.

Result on Karmic lines: every Hypnotist, every man of Science, however well-meaning and honorable, once he has allowed himself to become the unconscious instructor of one who learns but to abuse the sacred science, becomes, of course, morally the confederate of every crime committed by this means.

Such is the consequence of public 'Hypnotic' experiments which thus lead to, and virtually are, BLACK MAGIC.

THE SIGNS OF THE TIMES

IT is intensely interesting to follow season after season the rapid evolution and change of public thought in the direction of the mystical. The educated mind is most undeniably attempting to free itself from the heavy fetters of materialism. The ugly caterpillar is writhing in the agonies of death, under the powerful efforts of the psychic butterfly to escape from its science-built prison, and every day brings some new glad tidings of one or more such mental births to light.

As the New York *Path* truly remarks in its September issue, when "Theosophical and kindred topics . . . are made the texts for novels," and, we may add, scientific essays and *brochures,* "the implication is that interest in them has become diffused through all social ranks." That kind of literature is "paradoxically proof that Occultism has passed beyond the region of careless amusement and entered that of serious inquiry." The reader has but to throw a retrospective glance at the publications of the last few years to find that such topics as Mysticism, Magic, Sorcery, Spiritualism, Theosophy, Mesmerism, or, as it is now called, Hypnotism, all the various branches in short of the *Occult* side of nature, are becoming predominant in every kind of literature. They visibly increase in proportion to the efforts made to discredit the movements in the cause of truth, and strangle inquiry—whether on the field of theosophy or spiritualism—by trying to besmear their most prominent heralds, pioneers, and defenders, with tar and feathers.

The key-note for mystic and Theosophic literature was Marion Crawford's *Mr. Isaacs.* It was followed by his *Zoroaster.* Then followed *The Romance of Two Worlds, by* Marie Corelli; R. Louis Stevenson's *Dr. Jekyll and Mr. Hyde; The Fallen Idol,* by Anstey; *King Solomon's Mines* and the thrice famous *She,* by H. Rider Haggard; *Affinities,* and *The Brother of the Shadow,* by Mrs. Campbell Praed; Edmund Downey's *House of Tears;* and many others less noticeable. And now there comes a fresh outburst in Florence Marryat's *Daughter of the Tropics,* and F. C. Philip's *Strange Adventures of Lucy Smith.* It is unnecessary to mention in detail the literature produced by avowed theosophists and occultists, some of whose works are very remarkable, while others are positively scientific, such as S. L. Macgregor Mather's *Kabbalah Unveiled,* and Dr. F. Hartmann's Para*celsus, Magic White and Black, etc. We* have also to note the fact that theosophy has now crossed the Channel, and is making its way into French literature. *La France* publishes a strange romance by Ch. Chincholle, pregnant with theosophy, occultism and mesmerism, and called La *Grand Prêtresse,* while *La Revue politique et litteraire* (19 February, 1887, *et seq.)* contained over the signature of Th. Bentzon, a novel called *Etnancipee,* wherein esoteric doctrines and adepts are mentioned in conjunction with the names of well-known theosophists. A sign of the times!

Literature—especially in countries free from government censorship—is the public heart and pulse. Besides the glaring fact that were there no demand there would be no supply, current literature is produced only to please, and is therefore evidently the mirror which faithfully reflects the state of the public mind. True, conservative editors, and their submissive correspondents and reporters, still go on slashing occasionally in print the fair faces of mystic spiritualism and theosophy, and some of them are still found, from time to time, indulging in a *brutal* personal attack. But they do no harm on the whole, except perhaps to their own editorial reputations, as such editors can never be suspected of an exuberance of culture and good taste after certain ungentlemanly personal attacks. They do good, on the contrary. For, while the theosophists and spiritualists so attacked may view the Billingsgate poured upon them in a true Socratean spirit, and console themselves with the knowledge that none of the epithets used can possibly apply to them, on the other hand, *too much* abuse and vilification generally ends by awakening the public sympathy for the victim; in the right-minded and impartial, at any rate.

In England people seem to like fair play, on the whole. It is not *bashi-bazouk*-like actions, the doughty deeds of those who delight in mutilating the slain and the wounded, that can find sympathy for any great length of time with the public. If—as maintained by our lay enemies and repeated by some *naïf* and too sanguine missionary organs—Spiritualism and Theosophy are "dead as a door-nail," *(sic!—vide* American Christian periodicals),—aye, "dead and buried," why, in such case, good Christian fathers, not leave the dead at rest till "Judgment Day"? And if they are not, then editors—the profane as well as the clerical—why should you still fear? Do not show yourselves such cowards if you have the truth on your side. *Magna est veritas et prevalebit,* and "murder will out," as it always has, sooner or later. Open your columns to *free* and fearless discussion, and do as the theosophical periodicals have ever done, and as *Lucifer* is now preparing to do. The 'bright Son of the morning' fears no light. He courts it, and is prepared to publish any inimical contributions (couched, of course, in decent language), however much at variance with his theosophical views. He is determined to give a fair hearing in any and every case, to both contending parties, and allow things and thoughts to be judged on their respective merits. For why, or what should one dread when fact and truth are one's only aim? *Du choc des opinions jaillit la verité* was said by a French philosopher. If Theosophy and Spiritualism are no better than "gigantic fraud and will-o'-the-wisps of the age" why such *expensive* crusades against both? And if they are not, why should Agnostics and searchers after truth in general, help bigoted and narrow-minded materialists, sectarians and dogmatists to hide our light under a bushel by mere brutal force and usurped authority? It is easy to surprise the good faith of the fair-minded. Still easier to discredit that which, by its intrinsic strangeness, is already unpopular and could hardly be credited in its palmiest days. "We welcome no supposition so eagerly as one which accords with and intensifies our own prejudices," says, in *Don Jesualdo,* a popular author. Therefore, *facts* become often cunningly concocted 'frauds,' and self-evident, glaring lies are accepted as gospel truths at the first breeze of Don Basilio's *Calumnia,* by those to whose hard-crusted preconceptions such slander is like heavenly dew.

But, beloved enemies, 'the light of Lucifer' may, after all, dispel some of the surrounding darkness. The mighty roaring voice of denunciation, so welcome to those whose little spites and hates and mental stagnation in the grasp of the social respectability it panders to, may yet be silenced by the voice of truth—"the still small voice"—whose destiny it ever was to first preach in the desert. That cold and artificial light which still seems to shine so dazzlingly over the alleged iniquities of professional mediums and the supposed sins of commission and omission of *non-professional* experimentalists, of free and independent theosophists, may yet be extinguished at the height of all its glory. For it is not quite the perpetual lamp of

37

the alchemist-philosopher. Still less is it that "light which never shone on sea or land," that ray of divine intuition, the spark which glimmers latent in the spiritual, never-erring perceptions of man or woman, and which is now awakening—for its time is at hand. A few years more, and the Aladdin's lamp, which called forth the ministering genius thereof, who, making three salutes to the public, proceeded forthwith to devour mediums and theosophists, like a juggler who swallows swords at a village fair, will get out of order. Its light, over which the anti-theosophists are crowing victory to this day, shall get dim. And then, perhaps, it will be discovered that what was claimed as a direct ray from the source of eternal truth was no better than a penny rush-light, in whose deceitful smoke and soot people got hypnotized, and saw everything upside down. It will be found that the hideous monsters of fraud and imposture had no existence outside the murky and dizzied brains of the Aladdins on their journey of discovery. And that, finally, the good people who listened to them, had been all the time seeing sights and hearing things under unconscious and mutual *suggestion*.

This is a scientific explanation, and requires no black magicians or *dugpas* at work; for 'suggestion' as now practised by the sorcerers of science is—*dugpaship* itself, *pur sang*. No Eastern ' adept of the *left* hand ' can do more mischief by his infernal art than a grave hypnotizer of the Faculty of Medicine, a disciple of Charcot, or of any other scientific *light* of the first magnitude. In Paris, as in St. Petersburg, crimes have been committed under 'suggestion.' Divorces have occurred, and husbands have nearly killed their wives and their supposed co-respondents, owing to tricks played on innocent and respectable women, who have thus had their fair name and all their future life blasted for ever. A son, under such influence, broke open the desk of on avaricious father, who caught him in the act, and nearly shot him in a fit of rage. One of the keys of Occultism is in the hands of science—cold, heartless, materialistic, and crassly ignorant of the other truly psychic side of the phenomenon: hence, powerless to draw a line of demarcation between the physiological and the purely spiritual effects of the disease inoculated, and unable to prevent future results and consequences of which it has no knowledge, and over which it has, therefore, no control.

We find in the *Lotus* of September, 1887, the following.—

A French paper, the *Paris,* for August 12th, contains a long and excellent article by G. Montorgueil, entitled, *The Accursed Sciences,* from which we extract the following passage, since we are, unfortunately, unable to quote the whole:—

"Some months ago, already, in I forget what case, the question of 'suggestion' was raised and taken account of by the judges. We shall certainly see people in the dock accused of occult malpractices. But how will the prosecution go to work? What arguments will it bring to bear? The crime by 'suggestion' is the ideal of a crime without proof. In such a case the gravest charges will never be more than presumptions, and fugitive presumptions. On what fragile scaffolding of suspicions will the charge rest? No examination, but a moral one, will be possible. We shall have to resign ourselves to hearing the Solicitor-general say to the accused: 'Accused, it appears from a perquisition made into your brain, etc.'

"Ah, the poor jurymen! it is they who are to be pitied. Taking their task to heart, they already have the greatest difficulty in separating the true from the false, even in rough and ready cases, the facts of which are obvious, all the details of which are tangible and the responsibilities clear. And we are going to ask them on their soul and conscience to decide questions of black magic! Verily their reason will not hold out through the fortnight; it will give way before that and sink into thaumaturgy.

"We move fast. The strange trials for sorcery will blossom anew; somnambules who were merely grotesque will appear in a tragic light; the coffee grounds, which so far only risked the police court, will hear their sentence at the assizes. The evil eye will figure among criminal offenses. These last years of the XIXth century will have seen us step from progress to progress, till we reach at last this judicial enormity: a second Laubardemont prosecuting another Urbain Grandier."

Serious, scientific, and political papers are full of earnest discussions on the subject. A St. Petersburg 'Daily' has a long *feuilleton* on the 'Bearing of *Hypnotic Suggestions* upon Criminal Law." "Cases of Hypnotism with criminal motives have of late begun to increase in an ever progressing ratio," it tells its readers. And it is not the only newspaper, nor is Russia the only country where the same tale is told. Careful investigations and researches have been made by distinguished lawyers and medical authorities. Data have been assiduously collected and have revealed that the curious phenomenon—which sceptics have hitherto derided, and young people have included among their evening *petits jeux innocents*—is a new and terrible danger to state and society.

Two facts have now become patent to law and science:—

(I) *That, in the perceptions of the hypnotized subject, the visionary representations called forth by 'suggestion,' become real existing actualities, the subject being, for the moment, the automatic executor of the will of the hypnotizes; and—*

(II) *That the great majority of persons experimented upon, are subject to hypnotic suggestion.*

Thus Liébeault found only *sixty* subjects intractable out of the *seven hundred* he experimented upon; and Bernheim, out of 1014 subjects, failed with only *twenty-six*. The field for the natural-born *jadoo-wala* (sorcery-mongers) is vast indeed! Evil has acquired a playground on which it may now exercise its sway upon many a generation of unconscious victims. For crimes undreamt of in the waking state, and felonies of the blackest dye, are now invited and encouraged by the new 'accursed science.' The real perpetrators of these deeds of darkness may now remain for ever hidden from the vengeance of human justice. The hand which executes the criminal suggestion is only that of an irresponsible automaton, whose memory preserves no trace of it, and who, moreover, is a witness who can easily be disposed of by compulsory suicide—again under 'suggestion.' What better means than these could be offered to the fiends of lust and revenge, to those dark Powers called human passions—ever on the lookout to break the universal commandment: 'Thou shalt not steal, nor murder, nor lust after thy neighbor's wife.' Liébeault *suggested* to a young girl that she should poison herself with prussic acid, and she swallowed the supposed drug without one moment's hesitation; Dr. Liégois *suggested* to a young woman that she owed him 5000 francs, and the subject forthwith signed a check for the amount. Bernheim *suggested* to another hysterical girl a long and complicated vision with regard to a criminal case. Two days after, although the hypnotizer had not exercised any new pressure upon her in the interim, she repeated distinctly the whole suggested story to a lawyer sent to her for the purpose. Had her evidence been seriously accepted, it would have brought the accused to the guillotine.

These cases present two dark and terrible aspects. From the moral standpoint, such processes and *suggestions* leave an indelible stain upon the purity of the subject's nature. Even the innocent mind of a ten year old child can thus be inoculated with vice, the poison-germ of which will develop in subsequent life.

On the judicial aspect it is needless to enter in great detail. Suffice it to say that it is this characteristic feature of the hypnotic state—the absolute surrender of will and self-consciousness to the hypnotizer—which possesses such importance, from its bearing upon crime, in the eyes of legal authorities. For if the hypnotizer has the subject entirely at his beck and call, so that he can cause him to commit any crime, acting, so to say, invisibly within him, then what are not the terrible 'judicial mistakes' to be expected? What wonder then, that the jurisprudence of one country after another has taken alarm, and is devising, one after the other, measures for repressing the exercise of hypnotism! In Denmark it has just been forbidden. Scientists have experimented upon sensitives with so much success that a hypnotized victim has been jeered and hooted through the streets on his way to commit a crime, which he would have completed unconsciously, had not the victim been warned beforehand by the hypnotizer.

In Brussels a recent and sad case is well-known to all. A young girl of good family was seduced while in a hypnotized state by a man who had first subjected her to his influence at a social gathering. She only realized her condition a few months later, when her relatives, who divined the criminal, forced her seducer to make the only possible reparation—that of marrying his victim.

The French. Academy has just been debating the question:—how far a hypnotized subject, from a mere victim, can become a regular tool of crime. Of course, no jurist or legislator can remain indifferent to this question; and it was averred that the crimes committed under *suggestion are* so unprecedented that some of them can hardly be brought within the scope of the law. Hence the prudent legal prohibition, just adopted in France, which enacts that no person, save those legally qualified to exercise the medical profession, shall hypnotize any other person. Even the physician who enjoys such legal right is permitted to hypnotize a person only in the presence of another qualified medical man, and with the written permission of the subject. Public *séances* of hypnotism are forbidden, and they are strictly confined to medical *cliniques* and laboratories. Those who break this law are liable to a heavy fine and imprisonment.

But the keynote has been struck, and many are the ways in which this *black art* may be used—laws notwithstanding. That it will be so used, the vile passions inherent in human nature are sufficient guarantee.

Many and strange will be the romances yet enacted; for truth is often stranger than fiction, and what is thought fiction is still more often truth.

No wonder then that occult literature is growing with every day. Occultism and sorcery are in the air, with no true philosophical knowledge to guide the experimenters and thus check evil results. 'Works of *fiction,*' the various novels and romances are called. 'Fiction' in the arrangement of their characters and the adventures of their heroes and heroines—admitted. Not so, as to the *facts* presented. These are *no fictions,* but true *presentiments* of what lies in the bosom of the future, and much of which is already born—nay corroborated by *scientific* experiments. Sign of the times! Close of a psychic cycle! The time for phenomena with, or through mediums, whether professional or otherwise, is gone by. It was the early season of the blossoming, of the era mentioned even in the Bible[1]; the tree of Occultism is now preparing for 'fruiting,' and the Spirit of the Occult is awakening in the blood of the new generations. If the old men only 'dream dreams,' the young ones already see visions,[2] and—record them in novels and works of fiction. Woe to the ignorant and the unprepared, and those who listen to the sirens of materialistic science! For indeed, indeed, many will be the unconscious crimes committed, and many will be the victims who will innocently suffer death by hanging and decapitation at the hands of the righteous judges and the *too innocent* jurymen, both alike ignorant of the fiendish power of 'SUGGESTION.'

---

[1] "It shall come to pass that I will pour out my Spirit upon all flesh; your sons and your daughters shall prophesy; your old men shall dream dreams; your young men shall see visions." (Joel ii, 28.)

[2] It is curious to note that Mr. Louis Stevenson, one of the most powerful of our imaginative writers, stated recently to a reporter that he is in the habit of constructing the plots of his tales in *dreams,* and among others that of Dr. Jekyll. "I dreamed," he continued, "the story of *Olalla* . . . and I have at the present moment two unwritten stories which I have likewise dreamed. . . . Even when fast asleep I know that it is I who am inventing." . . . But who knows whether the idea of "invention" is not also a "dream"!

STUDIES IN OCCULTISM

A Series of Reprints from the Writings

of

H. P. BLAVATSKY

NO. III

PSYCHIC AND NOETIC ACTION

PSYCHIC AND NOETIC ACTION

... I made man just and right, Sufficient to have stood, though free to fall, Such I
created all th' ethereal powers
And spirits, both them who stood and them who fail'd,
Truly, they stood who stood, and fell who fell.

—Milton

"The assumption that the *mind is a real being,* which can be acted upon by the brain, and which
can act on the body through the brain, is the only one compatible with all the facts of experience.—
George T. Ladd, in the *Elements of Physiological Psychology*".

I

A NEW influence, a breath, a sound—"as of a rushing mighty wind"—has suddenly
swept over a few Theosophical heads. An idea, vague at first, grew in time into a
very definite form, and now seems to be working very busily in the minds of some
of our members. It is this: if we would make converts, the few ex-occult teachings,
which are destined to see the light of publicity, should be made, henceforward,
more subservient to, if not entirely at one with modern science. It is urged that the
so-called *esoteric*[1] (or *late* esoteric) cosmogony, anthropology, ethnology, ge-
ology—psychology and foremost of all, metaphysics—having been *adapted into*
making obeisance to modern (hence *materialistic)* thought, should never
henceforth be allowed to contradict (not *openly,* at all events) "scientific
philosophy." The latter, we suppose, means the fundamental and accepted views of
the great German schools, or of Mr. Herbert Spencer and some other English stars
of lesser magnitude; and not only these, but also the deductions that may be drawn
from them by their more or less instructed disciples.

A large undertaking this, truly; and one, more-over, in perfect conformity with
the policy of the medieval Casuists, who distorted truth and even suppressed it, if
it clashed with *divine Revelation.* Useless to say that we decline the compromise.
It is quite possible—nay, probable and almost unavoidable—that "the mistakes
made" in the rendering of such abstruse metaphysical tenets as those contained in
Eastern Occultism, should be "frequent and often important." But then all such
have to be traced back to the interpreters, not to the system itself. They have to be
corrected on the authority of the same Doctrine, checked by the teachings grown
on the rich and steady soil of *Guptâ-Vidyâ,* not by the speculations that blossom
forth today, to die tomorrow—on the shifting sands of modern scientific guess-
work, especially in all that relates to psychology and mental phenomena. Holding
to our motto, "There is no religion higher than truth," we refuse most decidedly to
pander to *physical* science. Yet, we may say this: If the so-called *exact* sciences
limited their activity only to the physical realm of nature; if they concerned
themselves strictly with surgery, chemistry—up to its legitimate boundaries, and
with physiology—so far as the latter relates to the structure of our corporeal frame,
then the Occultists would be the first to seek help in modern sciences, however
many their blunders and mistakes. But once that over-stepping material Nature the
physiologists of the modern "animalistic"[2] school pretend to meddle with, and

---

[1] We say "so-called," because nothing of what has been given out publicly or in print can any longer be
termed *esoteric.*

[2] "Animalism" is quite an appropriate word to use (whoever invented it) as a contrast to Mr. Tylor's
term "animism," which he applied to all the *"Lower* Races" of mankind who believe the soul a distinct

43

deliver *ex cathedra dicta* on, the higher functions and phenomena of the mind, saying that a careful analysis brings them to a firm conviction that no more than the animal is man a *free-agent,* far less a responsible one—then the Occultist has a far greater right than the average modern "Idealist" to protest. And the Occultist asserts that no materialist—a prejudiced and one-sided witness at best—can claim any authority in the question of mental physiology, or that which is now called by him the *physiology of the soul.* No such noun can be applied to the word "soul," unless, indeed, by soul only the lower, *psychic* mind is meant, or that which develops in man (proportionally with the perfection of his brain) into *intellect,* and in the animal into a *higher* instinct. But since the great Charles Darwin taught that "our *ideas are* animal motions of the organ of sense" everything becomes possible to the modern physiologist.

Thus, to the great distress of our scientifically inclined Fellows, it is once more *Lucifer's* duty to show how far we are at logger-heads with exact science, or shall we say, how far the conclusions of that science are drifting away from truth and fact. By "science" we mean, of course, the majority of the men of science; the best minority, we are happy to say, is on our side, at least as far as free-will in man and the immateriality of the mind are concerned. The study of the "Physiology" of the Soul, of the Will in man and of his *higher Consciousness* from the standpoint of genius and its manifesting faculties, can never be summarized into a system of general ideas represented by brief formulae; no more than the *psychology of material nature* can have its manifold mysteries solved by the mere analysis of its physical phenomena. *There is no special organ of will,* any more than there is a *physical basis* for the activities of self-consciousness.

"If the question is pressed as to the *physical basis* for the activities of self-consciousness, no answer can be given or suggested. . . . From its very nature, that marvelous verifying *actus* of mind in which it recognizes the states as its own, can have no analogous or corresponding material substratum. It is impossible to specify any physiological process representing this unifying *actus;* it is even impossible to imagine how the description of any such process could be brought into intelligible relation with this unique mental power."[1]

Thus the whole conclave of psycho-physiologists may be challenged to correctly define Consciousness, and they are sure to fail, because Self-consciousness belongs alone to man and proceeds from the SELF, the higher Manas. Only, whereas the psychic element (or *Kama Manas*)[2] is common to both the animal and the human being—the far higher degree of its development in the latter resting merely on the greater perfection and sensitiveness of his cerebral cells—no physiologist, not even the cleverest, will ever be able to solve the mystery of the human mind, in its higher spiritual manifestation, or in its dual

---

entity. He finds that the words *psyche, pneuma, animus, spiritus, etc.,* all belong to the same cycle of superstition in "the lower stages of culture," Professor A. Bain dubbing all these distinctions, moreover, as a "plurality of souls" and a "double materialism." This is the more curious as the learned author of *Mind and Body* speaks as disparagingly of Darwin's "materialism" in *Zoonomia,* wherein the founder of modern Evolution defines the word *idea* as "contracting a motion, or configuration of the fibers which constitute the immediate organ of. Sense". ("Mind and Body", p. 190, Note.)
[1] *Physiological Psychology, etc.,* p. 545, by George T. Ladd, Professor of Philosophy in Yale University.
[2] Or what the Kabalists call *Nephesh,* the "breath of life."

aspect of the *psychic* and the *noetic* (or the *manasic),*[1] or even to comprehend the intricacies of the former on the purely material plane—unless he knows something of, and is prepared to admit the presence of this dual element. This means that he would have to admit a lower (animal), and a higher (or divine) mind in man, or what is known in Occultism as the "personal" and the "impersonal" *Egos.* For, between the *psychic* and the *noetic,* between the *Personality* and the *Individuality,* there exists the same abyss as between a "Jack the Ripper," and a holy Buddha. Unless the physiologist accepts all this, we say, he will ever be led into a quagmire. We intend to prove it.

As all know, the great majority of our learned "Didymi" reject the idea of free-will. Now this question is a problem that has occupied the minds of thinkers for ages; every school of thought having taken it up in turn and left it as far from solution as ever. And yet, placed as it is in the foremost ranks of philosophical quandaries, the modern "psycho-physiologists" claim in the coolest and most bumptious way to have cut the Gordian knot forever. For them the feeling of personal free agency is an error, an illusion, "the collective hallucination of mankind." This conviction starts from the principle that no mental activity is possible without a brain, and that there can be no brain without a body. As the latter is, moreover, subject to the general laws of a material world where all is based on necessity, and where there is no spontaneity, our modern psycho-physiologist has *nolens volens* to repudiate any self-spontaneity in human action. Here we have, for instance, a Lausanne professor of physiology, A. A. Herzen, to whom the claim of free-will in man appears as the most *unscientific* absurdity. Says this oracle:

"In the boundless physical and chemical laboratory that surrounds man, organic life represents quite an unimportant group of phenomena; and amongst the latter, the place occupied by life having reached to the stage of consciousness, is so minute that it is absurd to exclude man from the sphere of action of a general law, in order to allow in him the existence of a subjective spontaneity or a free will standing outside of that law".— (*Psychophysiologie Generale.*)

For the Occultist who knows the difference between the psychic and the noetic elements in man, this is pure trash, notwithstanding its sound scientific basis. For when the author puts the question—if psychic phenomena do not represent the results of an action of a molecular character whither then does motion disappear after reaching the sensory centres?—we answer that we never denied the fact. But what has this to do with a free-will? That every phenomenon in the visible Universe has its genesis in motion, is an old axiom in Occultism; nor do we doubt that the psycho-physiologist would place himself at logger-heads with the whole conclave of exact scientists were he to allow the idea that at a given moment a whole series of physical phenomena may disappear in the vacuum. Therefore, when the author of the work cited maintains that the said force does not disappear upon reaching the highest nervous centres, but that it is forthwith transformed into another series, *viz.,* that of psychic manifestations, into thought, feeling, and consciousness, just as this same psychic force when applied to produce some work of a physical (*e.g.,* muscular) character gets transformed into the latter—Occultism

---

[1] The Sanskrit word *Manas* (Mind) is used by us in preference to the Greek *Nous* (noetic) because the latter word having been so imperfectly understood in philosophy, suggests no definite meaning.

supports him, for it is the first to say that all psychic activity, from its lowest to its highest manifestations, is "nothing but—motion."

Yes, it is MOTION; but not all "molecular" motion, as the writer means us to infer. Motion as the GREAT BREATH (*vide* "Secret Doctrine", vol. I, *sub voce*)—*ergo* "*sound*" at *the same time*—is the substratum of Kosmic-Motion. It is beginningless and endless, the one *eternal life,* the basis and genesis of the subjective and the objective universe; for LIFE (or Be-ness) is the *fons et origo* of existence or being. But molecular motion is the lowest and most material of its finite manifestations. And if the general law of the conservation of energy leads modern science to the conclusion that psychic activity only represents a special form of motion, this same law, guiding the Occultists, leads them also to the same conviction—and to something else besides, which psycho-physiology leaves entirely out of all consideration. If the latter has discovered only in this century[1] that psychic (we say even spiritual) action is subject to the same general and immutable laws of motion as any other phenomenon manifested in the objective realm of Kosmos, and that in both the organic and the *inorganic* (?) worlds every manifestation, whether conscious or unconscious, represents but the result of a collectivity of causes, then in Occult philosophy this represents merely the A, B, C, of its science. "All the world is in the *swara; swara* is the Spirit itself"—the ONE LIFE or *motion,* say the old books of Hindiu Occult philosophy. "The proper translation of the word *swara* is the *current of the life wave,"* says the author of "Nature's Finer Forces",[2] and he goes on to explain:—

"It is that wavy motion which is the cause of the evolution of cosmic undifferentiated matter into the differentiated universe, . From whence does this motion come? This motion is the spirit itself. The word *atman* (universal soul) used in the book (*vide infra),* itself carries the idea of eternal motion, coming as it does from the root AT, eternal motion; and, it may be significantly remarked, that the root AT is connected with, is in fact simply another form of, the roots AH, breath, and As, being. All these roots have for their origin the sound produced by the breath of animals (living beings). . . . The primeval current of the life-wave is then the same which assumes in man the form of the inspiratory and expiratory motion of the lungs, and this is the all-pervading source of the evolution and involution of the universe. . . ."

So much about *motion* and the "conservation of energy" from old *books on magic* written and taught ages before the birth of inductive and exact modern science. For what does the latter say more than these books in speaking, for instance, about animal *mechanism,* when it says:

"From the visible atom to the celestial body lost in space, *everything is subject to motion* . . . kept at a definite distance one from the other, in proportion to the motion which animates them, the molecules present constant relations, which they lose only by the

---

[1] *Ed.,* 19th
[2] *The Theosophist,* Feb. 1888, p. 275, by Rama Prasad, President of the *Meerut Theosophical Society.* As the Occult book cited by him says: "It is the *Swara* that has given form to the first *accumulations of the divisions* of the universe; the *Swara* causes evolution and involution; the *Swara* is God, or more properly the *Great Power* itself *(Maheshwara).* The *Swara* is the manifestation of the impression on matter of that power which in man is known to us as *the power which knows itself* [mental and *psychic* consciousness]. It is to be understood that the action of this power never ceases. . . . It is unchangeable existence"—and this is the "Motion" of the Scientists and the universal *Breath of Life* of the Occultists.

46

addition or the subtraction of a certain quantity of motion".[1]

But Occultism says more than this. While making of motion *on the material plane* and of the conservation of energy, two fundamental laws, or rather two aspects of the same omnipresent law—*Swara,* it denies point blank that these have anything to do with *free-will in* man, which belongs to quite a different plane. The author of "Psychophysiologie Generale", treating of his *discovery* that psychic action is but motion, and the result of a collectivity of causes—remarks that as it is so, there cannot be any further discussion upon spontaneity—in the sense of any native internal proneness created by the human organism; and adds that the above puts an end to all claim for *free-will!* The Occultist denies the conclusion. The actual fact of man's psychic (we say *manasic* or noetic) *individuality is* a sufficient warrant against the assumption; for in the case of this conclusion being correct, or being indeed, as the author expresses it, the *collective hallucination of the whole mankind throughout the ages,* there would be an end also to psychic individuality.

Now by "psychic" individuality we mean that self-determining power which enables man to override circumstances. Place half a dozen animals of the same species under the same circumstances, and their actions, while not identical, will be closely similar; place half a dozen men under the same circumstances, and their actions will be as different as their characters, *i. e., psychic individuality.*

But if instead of "psychic" we call it the higher Self-conscious Will, then having been shown by the science of psycho-physiology itself that will has no *special organ,* how will the materialists connect it with "molecular" motion at all? As Professor George T. Ladd says:

"The phenomena of human *consciousness must be regarded as activities of some other form of Real Being, than the moving molecules of the* brain. They require a subject or ground which is in its nature unlike the phosphorized fats of the central masses, the aggregated nerve-fibres of nerve-cells of the cerebral cortex. This Real Being thus mani-fested immediately to itself in the phenomena of consciousness, and indirectly to others through the bodily changes, is the Mind (manas). To it the mental phenomena are to be attributed as showing what it is by what it *does.* The so-called mental 'faculties' are only the *modes of the behavior* in consciousness of this real being. We actually find, by the only method available, that this real being called Mind believes in certain perpetually recurring modes; therefore, we attribute to it certain faculties . . . Mental faculties are not entities that have an existence of themselves . . . They are the modes of the behavior in consciousness of the mind. And the very nature of the classifying acts which lead to their being distinguished, is explicable only upon the assumption that a *Real Being called Mind exists,* and is to be distinguished from the real beings known as the physical molecules of the brain's nervous mass.[2]*

And having shown that we have to regard consciousness *as a unit* (another occult proposition) the author adds:—

"We conclude, then, from the previous considerations: *the subject of all the states of consciousness is a real unit-being, called Mind; which is of nonmaterial nature, and acts and develops according to laws of its own, but is specially correlated with certain material*

---

[1] *Animal Mechanism, a treatise* on terrestrial *and aerial locomotion.* By E. J. Marcy, Professor at the College of France, and member of the Academy of Medicine.

[2] The higher maws or "Ego" *(Kshetrajna) is* the "Silent Spectator," and the voluntary "sacrificial victim": the lower manas, its representative—a tyrannical despot, truly.

molecules and masses forming the substance of the Brain".[1]

This "Mind" is manas, or rather its lower reflection, which whenever it disconnects itself, for the time being, from *kama,* becomes the guide of the highest mental faculties, and is the organ of the free-will in physical man. Therefore, this assumption of the newest psycho-physiology is uncalled for, and the apparent impossibility of reconciling the existence of free-will with the law of the conservation of energy is—a pure fallacy. This was well shown in the "Scientific Letters" of "Elpay" in a criticism of the work. But to prove it finally and set the whole question definitely at rest, does not even require so high an interference (high for us, at any rate) as the Occult laws, but simply a little common sense. Let us analyse the question dispassionately.

It is postulated by one man, presumably a scientist, that because "psychic action is found subject to the general and immutable laws of motion, there is, therefore, *no free-will in man.* " The "analytical method of exact sciences" has demonstrated it, and materialistic scientists have decreed to "pass the resolution" that the fact should be so accepted by their followers. But there are other and far greater scientists who thought differently. For instance, Sir William Lawrence, the eminent surgeon, declared in his lectures[2] that:—

"The philosophical doctrine of the soul, and its separate existence, has nothing to do with this physiological question, but rests on a species of proof altogether different. These sublime dogmas could never have been brought to light by the labors of the anatomist and the physiologist. An immaterial and spiritual being could not have been discovered amid the blood and filth of the dissecting room".

Now, let us examine on the testimony of the materialist how this universal solvent called the "analytical method" is applied in this special case. The author of *"Psychophysiologie"* decomposes psychic activity into its compound elements, traces them back to motion, and, failing to find in them the slightest trace of free-will or spontaneity, jumps at the conclusion that the latter have no existence in general; nor are they to be found in that psychic activity which he has just decomposed, "Are not the fallacy and error of such an unscientific proceeding self-evident?" asks his critic; and then argues very correctly that:—

"At this rate, and starting from the standpoint of this analytical method, one would have an equal right to deny every phenomenon in nature from first to last. For, do not sound and light, heat and electricity, like all other chemical processes, once decomposed into their respective elements, lead the experimenter back to the same motion, wherein all the peculiarities of the given elements disappear, leaving behind them only "the vibrations of molecules"? But does it necessarily follow that for all that, heat, light, electricity—are but illusions instead of the actual manifestations of the peculiarities of our real world? Such peculiarities are not, of course, to be found in compound elements, simply because we cannot expect that a part should contain, from first to last, the properties of the whole. What should we say of a chemist, who, having decomposed water into its compounds, hydrogen and oxygen, without finding in them the special characteristics of water, would maintain that such did not exist at all nor could they be found in water? What of an antiquary, who

---

[1] *Elements of Physiological Psychology.* A treatise on the activities and nature of the Mind, from the Physical and Experimental Point of View, pp. 606 and 613.
[2] W. Lawrence. *Lectures on Comparitive Anatomy, Physiology, Zoology, and the Natural History of Man.* 8vo. London, 1848, p. 6.

upon examining distributed type and finding no sense in every separate letter, should assert that there was no such thing as sense to be found in any printed document? And does not the author of *Psychophysiology* act just in this way when he denies the existence of free-will or self-spontaneity in man, on the grounds that this distinctive faculty of the highest psychic activity is absent from those compound elements which he has analysed?"

Most undeniably no separate piece of brick, of wood, or iron, each of which has once been a part of a building now in ruins, can be expected to preserve the smallest trace of the architecture of that building—in the hands of the chemist, at any rate; though it would in those of a *psychometer,* a faculty, by the bye, which demonstrates far more powerfully the law of the conservation of energy than any physical science does, and shows it acting as much in the subjective or psychic worlds as on the objective and material planes. The genesis of sound, on this plane, has to be traced back to the same motion, and the same correlation of forces is at play during the phenomenon as in the case of every other manifestation. Shall the physicist, then, who decomposes sound into its compound element of vibrations and fails to find in them any harmony or special melody, deny the existence of the latter? And does not this prove that the analytical method having to deal exclusively with the elements, and nothing to do with their *combinations,* leads the physicist to talk very glibly about motion, vibration, and what not, and to make him entirely lose sight of the *harmony produced by certain combinations of that motion* or the "harmony of vibrations"? Criticism, then, is right in accusing Materialistic psycho-physiology of neglecting these all-important distinctions; in maintaining that if a careful observation of facts is a duty in the simplest physical phenomena, how much more should it be so when applied to such complex and important questions as psychic force and faculties? And yet in most cases all such essential differences are overlooked, and the analytical method is applied in a most arbitrary and prejudiced way. What wonder, then, if, in carrying back psychic action to its basic elements of motion, the psycho-physiologist depriving it during the process of all its essential characteristics, should destroy it; and having destroyed it, it only stands to reason that he is unable to find that which exists in it no longer. He forgets, in short, or rather purposely ignores the fact, that though, like all other phenomena on the material plane, psychic manifestations must be related in their final analysis to the world of vibration *("sound" being the substratum of universal Akasa), yet,* in their origin, they belong to *a different and a higher World* of HARMONY. Elpay has a few severe sentences against the assumptions of those he calls "physico-biologists" which are worthy of note.

"Unconscious of their error, the psycho-physiologists identify the compound elements of psychic activity with that activity itself: hence the conclusion from the standpoint of the analytical method, that the highest, distinctive speciality of the human soul—free-will, spontaneity—is an illusion, and no psychic reality. But as we have just shown, such identification not only has nothing in common with exact science, but is simply impermissible, as it clashes with all the fundamental laws of logic, in consequence of which all these so-called physico-biological deductions emanating from the said identification vanish into thin air. Thus to trace psychic action primarily to motion, means in no way to prove the "illusion of free-will." And, as in the case of water, whose specific qualities cannot be deprived of their reality although they are not to be found in its compound gases, so with regard to the specific property of psychic action: its spontaneity cannot be refused to psychic reality, though this property is not contained in those finite elements into which the psycho-physiologist dismembers the activity in question under his mental scalpel."

This method is "a distinctive feature of modern science in its endeavor to satisfy inquiry into the *nature* of the objects of its investigation by a detailed description of their *development,*" says G. T. Ladd. And the author of "The Elements of Physiological Psychology," adds:—

"The universal process of 'Becoming' has been almost personified and deified so as to make it the true ground of all finite and concrete existence. . . The attempt is made to refer all the so-called development of the mind to the evolution of the substance of the brain, under purely physical and mechanical causes. This attempt, then, denies that any real unit-being called the Mind needs to be assumed as undergoing a process of development according to laws of its own. . . . On the other hand, all attempts to account for the orderly increase in complexity and comprehensiveness of the mental phenomena by tracing the physical evolution of the brain are wholly unsatisfactory to many minds. We have no hesitation in classing ourselves among this number. Those facts of experience which show a correspondence in the order of the development of the body and the mind, and even a certain necessary dependence of the latter upon the former, are, of course, to be admitted; but they are equally compatible with another view of the mind's development. This other view has the additional advantages that it makes room for many other facts of experience which are very difficult of reconciliation with any materialistic theory. On the whole, *the history of each individual's experiences is such as requires the assumption that a real unit-being (a Mind) is undergoing a process of development, in relation to the changing condition or evolution of the brain, and yet in accordance with a nature and laws of its own.* (p. 616)"

How closely this last "assumption" of science approaches the teachings of the Occult philosophy will be shown in Part II of this article. Meanwhile, we may close with an answer to the latest materialistic fallacy, which may be summarized in a few words. As every psychic action has for its subtratum the nervous elements whose existence it postulates, and outside which it cannot act; as the activity of the nervous elements are only molecular motion, there is therefore no need to invent a special and psychic Force for the explanation of our brain work. *Free-will would force* Science to postulate an invisible *Free-Willer,* a creator of that special Force.

We agree: "not the slightest need" of a creator of "that special" or any other Force. Nor has anyone ever claimed such an absurdity. But between *creating* and *guiding* there is a difference, and the latter implies in no way any creation of the energy of motion, or, indeed, of any special energy. *Psychic mind* (in contra-distinction to manasic or noetic mind) only transforms this energy of the "unit-being" according to "a nature and laws of its own"—to use Ladd's felicitous expression. The "unit-being" creates nothing, but only causes a natural correlation in accordance with both the physical laws and *laws of its own;* having to use the Force, it guides its direction, choosing the paths along which it will proceed, and stimulating it to action. And, as its activity is *sui generis,* and independent, it carries this energy from this world of disharmony into its own sphere of harmony. Were it not *independent* it could not do so. As it is, the freedom of man's will is beyond doubt or cavil. Therefore, as already observed, there is no question of creation, but simply of *guidance.* Because the sailor at the wheel does not create the steam in the engine, shall we say that he does not direct the vessel?

And, because we refuse to accept the fallacies of some psycho-physiologists as the *last* word of science, do we furnish thereby a new proof that free-will is a *hallucination?* We deride the *animalistic* idea. How far more scientific and logical, besides being as poetical as it is grand, is the teaching in the *Kathopanishad,* which, in a beautiful and descriptive metaphor, says that: "The senses are the horses, body is the chariot, mind *(kama-manas)* is the reins, and intellect (or *free-will)* the charioteer." Verily there is more *exact* science in the less important of the *Upanishads,* composed thousands of years ago, than in all the materialistic ravings of modern "physico-biology" and "psycho-physiology" put together!

". . . The knowledge of the past, present, and future is embodied in Kshetrajna (the 'Self')."— *Occult Axioms*

HAVING explained in what particulars, and why, as Occultists, we disagree with materialistic physiological psychology, we may now proceed to point out the difference between psychic and noetic mental functions, the noetic not being recognized by official science.

Moreover, we, Theosophists, understand the terms "psychic" and "psychism" somewhat differently from the average public, science, and even theology, the latter giving it a significance which both science and Theosophy reject, and the public in general remaining with a very hazy conception of what is really meant by the terms. For many, there is little, if any, difference between "psychic" and "psychological," both words relating in some way to the *human* soul. Some modern metaphysicians have wisely agreed to disconnect the word Mind *(pneuma)* from Soul *(psyche),* the one being the rational, spiritual part, the other—*psyche*—the living principle in man, the breath that *animates* him (from *anima, soul).* Yet, if this is so, how in this case refuse a soul to *animals?* These are, no less than man, informed with the same principle of sentient life, the *nephesh* of the 2d chapter of *Genesis.* The Soul is by no means the Mind, nor can an idiot, bereft of the latter, be called a "soul-less" being. To describe, as the physiologists do, the human Soul in its relation to senses and appetites, desires and passions, common to man and the brute, and then endow it with God-like intellect, with spiritual and rational faculties which can take their source but in a *supersensible* world—is to throw forever the veil of an impenetrable mystery over the subject. Yet in modern science, "psychology" and "psychism" relate only to conditions of the nervous system, mental phenomena being traced solely to molecular action. The higher *noetic* character of the Mind-Principle is entirely ignored, and even rejected as "superstition" by both physiologists and psychologists. Psychology, in fact, has become a synonym in many cases for the science of psychiatry. Therefore, students of Theosophy being compelled to differ from all these, have adopted the doctrine that underlies the time-honored philosophies of the East. What it is, may be found further on.

To better understand the foregoing arguments and those which follow, the reader is asked to turn to the editorial in the September *Lucifer,* ("The Dual Aspect of Wisdom," p. 3) and acquaint himself with the *double aspect* of that which is termed by St. James in his Third Epistle—at once—the *devilish, terrestrial,* wisdom, and the "wisdom from above." In another editorial, "Kosmic Mind" (April, 1890), it is also stated that the ancient Hindus endowed every cell in the human body with consciousness, giving each the name of a God or Goddess. Speaking of atoms in the name of science and philosophy, Professor Ladd calls them in his work *"supersensible beings."* Occultism regards every atom[1] as an "independent entity" and every cell as a "conscious unit." It explains that no sooner do such atoms group to form cells, than the latter become endowed with consciousness, each of its own kind, and with *free will to act within* the limits of the law. Nor are we entirely deprived of scientific evidence for such statements, as the two above named editorials well proved. More than one learned physiologist of the golden minority, in our own day, moreover, is rapidly coming to the conviction that memory has no seat, no special organ of its own in the human brain, but that it

---

[1] One of the names of Brahmâ is *anu* or "atom."

has *seats* in every organ of the body.

"No good ground exists for speaking of any special organ, or seat of memory," writes Professor G. T. Ladd. "Every organ, indeed every area, and every limit of the nervous system has its own memory." (p. 553, *loc. cit.*).

The seat of memory, then, is assuredly %either here nor there, but everywhere throughout the human body. To locate its organ in the brain is to limit and dwarf the Universal Mind and its countless Rays (the *Manasa putra*) which inform every rational mortal. As we write for Theosophists, first of all, we care little for the psychophobian prejudices of the Materialists who may read this and sniff contemptuously at the mention of "Universal Mind," and the Higher *noetic* souls of men. But, what *is* memory?—we ask. "Both presentation of sense and image of memory, are transitory phases of consciousness," we are answered. But what is Consciousness itself?—we ask again. *"We cannot define Consciousness,"* Professor Ladd tells us.[1] Thus that which we are asked to do by physiological psychology is, to content ourselves with controverting the various states of Consciousness by other people's private and unverifiable hypotheses; and this, on "questions of cerebral physiology *where experts and novices are alike ignorant,"* to use the pointed remark of the said author. Hypothesis for hypothesis, then, we may as well hold to the teachings of our Seers, as to the conjectures of those who deny both such Seers and their wisdom. The more so, as we are told by the same honest man of science, that "if metaphysics and ethics cannot properly dictate their facts and conclusions to the science of physiological psychology. . . in turn this science cannot properly dictate to metaphysics and ethics the conclusions which they shall draw from facts of Consciousness, by giving out its myths and fables in the garb of well ascertained history of the cerebral processes." (p. 554).

Now, since the metaphysics of Occult physiology and psychology postulate within mortal man an immortal entity, "divine Mind," or *Nous,* whose pale and too often distorted reflection is that which we call "Mind" and intellect in men— virtually an entity apart from the former during the period of every incarnation— we say that the *two* sources of "memory" are in these two "principles." These two we distinguish as the Higher *Manas* (Mind or Ego), and the *Kama-Manas, i.e.,* the rational, but earthly or physical intellect of man, incased in, and bound by, matter, therefore subject to the influence of the latter: the all-conscious SELF, that which reincarnates periodically—verily the WORD made flesh!—and which is always the same, while its reflected "Double," changing with every new incarnation and personality, is, therefore, conscious but for a life-period. The latter "principle" is the *Lower* Self, or that which, manifesting through our *organic* system, acting on this plane of illusion, imagines itself the *Ego Sum,* and thus falls into what Buddhist philosophy brands as the "heresy of separateness." The former we term INDIVIDUALITY, the latter *Personality.* From the first proceeds all the *noetic* element, from the second, the *psychic, i.e.,* "terrestrial wisdom" at best, as it is influenced by all the chaotic stimuli of the human or rather *animal passions* of the living body.

The "Higher Ego" cannot act directly on the body, as its consciousness belongs to quite another plane and planes of ideation: the "lower" *Self* does: and its action and behavior *depend on its free-will and choice as* to whether it will gravitate

---

[1] *Elements of Physiological Psychology.*

more towards its parent ("the Father in Heaven") or the "animal" which it informs, the man of flesh. The "Higher Ego," as part of the essence of the UNIVERSAL MIND, is unconditionally omniscient on its own plane, and only potentially so in our terrestrial sphere, as it has to act solely through its *alter ego*—the Personal Self. Now, although the former is the vehicle of all knowledge of the past, the present, and the future, and although it is from this fountain-head that its "double" catches occasional glimpses of that which is beyond the senses of man, and transmits them to certain brain cells (unknown to science in their functions), thus making of man a *Seer*, a soothsayer, and a prophet; yet the memory of bygone events—especially of the earth earthy—has its seat in the Personal Ego alone. No memory of a purely daily-life function, of a physical, egotistical, or of a lower mental nature—such as, *e.g.*, eating and drinking, enjoying personal sensual pleasures, transacting business to the detriment of one's neighbor, etc., etc., has aught to do with the "Higher" Mind or Ego. Nor has it any direct dealings on this physical plane with either our brain or our heart for these two are the organs of a power higher than the *Personality*—but only with our passional organs, such as the liver, the stomach, the spleen, etc. Thus it only stands to reason that the memory of such-like events must be first awakened in that organ which was the first to induce the action remembered afterwards, and conveyed it to our "sense-thought," which is entirely *distinct from the "super-sensuous" thought*. It is only the higher forms of the latter, the *superconscious* mental experiences, that can correlate with the cerebral and cardiac centers. The memories of physical and *selfish* (or personal) deeds, on the other hand, together with the mental experiences of a terrestrial nature, and of earthly biological functions, can, of necessity, only be correlated with the molecular constitution of various *Kamic* organs, and the "dynamical associations" of the elements of the nervous system in each particular organ.

Therefore, when Professor Ladd, after showing that every element of the nervous system has a memory of its own, adds:—"This view belongs to the very essence of every theory which considers conscious mental reproduction as only one form or phase of the biological fact of organic memory"—he must include among such theories the Occult teaching. For no Occultist could express such teaching more correctly than the Professor, who says, in winding up his argument: "We might properly speak, then, of the memory of the end-organ of vision or of hearing, of the memory of the spinal cord and of the different so-called 'centers' of reflex action belonging to the cords, of the memory of the medulla oblongata, the cerebellum, etc." This is the essence of Occult teaching—even in the Tantra works. Indeed, every organ in our body *has its own memory*. For if it is endowed with a consciousness "of its own kind," every cell must of necessity have also a memory of its own kind, as likewise its own *psychic* and *noetic* action. Responding to the touch of both a physical and a *metaphysical* Force,[1] the impulse given by the *psychic* (or psycho-molecular) Force will act from *without within;* while that of the *noetic* (shall we call it Spiritual-dynamical?) Force works from *within without*. For, as our body is the covering of the inner "principles," soul, mind, life, etc., so the molecule or the cell is the body in which dwell its "principles," the (to our senses and comprehension) immaterial atoms which compose that cell. The cell's activity and behavior are determined by its being

---

[1] We fondly trust this very *unscientific term* will throw no "Animalist" into hysterics *beyond* recovery.

54

propelled either inwardly or outwardly by the noetic or the psychic Force, the former having no relation to the *physical* cells proper. Therefore, while the latter act under the unavoidable law of the conservation and correlation of physical energy, the atoms—being psycho-spiritual, *not physical units—act under laws of their own,* just as Professor Ladd's "Unit-Being," which is our "Mind-Ego," does, in his very philosophical and scientific hypothesis. Every human organ and each cell in the latter has a key-board of its own, like that of a piano, only that it registers and emits sensations instead of sounds. Every key contains the potentiality of good or bad, of producing harmony or disharmony. This depends on the impulse given and the combinations produced; on the force of the touch of the artist at work, a "double-faced Unity," indeed. And it is the action of this or the other "Face" of the Unity that determines the nature and the dynamical character of the manifested phenomena as a resulting action, and this whether they be physical or mental. For the whole life of man is guided by this double-faced Entity. If the impulse comes from the "Wisdom above," the Force applied being noetic or spiritual, the results will be actions worthy of the divine propeller; if from the "terrestrial, devilish wisdom" (psychic power), man's activities will be selfish based solely on the exigencies of his physical, hence animal, nature. The above may sound to the average reader as pure nonsense; but every Theosophist must understand when told that there are *Manasic* as well as *Kamic* organs in him, although the cells of his body answer to both physical and spiritual impulses.

Verily that body, so desecrated by Materialism and man himself, is the temple of the Holy Grail, the *Adytum* of the grandest, nay, of all, the mysteries of nature in our solar universe. That body is an Æolian harp, chorded with two sets of strings, one made of pure silver, the other of catgut. When the breath from the divine Fiat brushes softly over the former, man becomes like unto *his* God—but the other set feels it not. It needs the breeze of a strong terrestrial wind, impregnated with animal effluvia, to set its animal chords vibrating. It is the function of the physical, lower mind to act upon the physical organs and their cells; but, it is the higher mind *alone* which can influence the atoms interacting in those cells, which interaction is alone capable of exciting the brain, *via the spinal "center" cord,* to a mental representation of spiritual ideas far beyond any objects on this material plane. The phenomena of divine consciousness have to be regarded as activities of our mind on another and a higher plane, working through something less substantial than the moving molecules of the brain. They cannot be explained as the simple resultant of the cerebral physiological processes, as indeed the latter only condition them or give them a final form for purposes of concrete manifestation. Occultism teaches that the liver and the spleen cells are the most subservient to the action of our "personal" mind, the heart being the organ *par excellence* through which the "Higher" Ego acts—through the Lower Self.

Nor can the visions or memory of purely terrestrial events be transmitted directly through the mental perceptions of the brain—the direct recipient of the impressions of the heart. All such recollections have to be first stimulated by and awakened in the organs which were the originators, as already stated, of the various causes that led to the results, or, the direct recipients and participators of the latter. In other words, if what is called "association of *ideas"* has much to do with the awakening of memory, the mutual interaction and consistent interrelation between the personal "Mind-Entity" and the organs of the human body have far more so. A hungry stomach evokes the vision of a past banquet, because its action is reflected and repeated in the *personal* mind. But even before the memory of the personal Self radiates the vision from the tablets wherein are stored the experiences of one's daily life—even to the minutest details—the memory of the stomach has already evoked the same. And so with all the organs of the body. It is they which originate according to their animal needs and desires the electro-vital sparks that illuminate the field of consciousness in the Lower Ego; and it is these sparks which in their turn awaken to function the reminiscences in it. The whole human body is, as said, a vast sounding board, in which each cell bears a long record of impressions connected with its parent organ, and each cell has a memory and a consciousness of its kind, or call it instinct if you will. These impressions are, according to the nature of the organ, physical, psychic, or mental, as they relate to this or another plane. They may be called "states of consciousness" only for the want of a better expression—as there are states of instinctual, mental, and purely abstract, or spiritual consciousness. If we trace all such "psychic" actions to brain-work, it is only because in that mansion called the human body the brain is the front-door, and the only one which opens out into Space. All the others are inner doors, openings in the private building, through which travel incessantly the transmitting agents of memory and sensation. The clearness, the vividness, and intensity of these depend on the state of health and the organic soundness of the transmitters. But their reality, in the sense of trueness or correctness, is due to the "principle" they originate from, and the preponderance in the Lower *Mona:* of the *noetic* or of the *phrenic* ("Kama," terrestrial) element.

For, as Occultism teaches, if the Higher Mind-Entity—the permanent and the immortal—is of the divine homogeneous essence of "Alaya-Akasa,"[1] or Mahat—its reflection, the Personal Mind, is, as a temporary "Principle," of the Substance of the Astral Light. As a pure ray of the "Son of the Universal Mind," it could perform no functions in the body, and would remain powerless over the turbulent organs of Matter. Thus, while its inner constitution is Manasic, its "body," or rather functioning essence, is heterogeneous, and leavened with the Astral Light, the lowest element of Ether. It is a part of the mission of the Manasic Ray, to get gradually rid of the blind, deceptive element which, though it makes of it an active spiritual entity on this plane, still brings it into so close contact with matter as to entirely becloud its divine nature and stultify its intuitions.

This leads us to see the difference between the purely noetic and the terrestrial psychic visions of seership and mediumship. The former can be obtained by one of two means: (*a*) on the condition of paralysing at will the *memory* and the instinctual, independent action of all the material organs and even cells in the body of flesh, an act which, once that the light of the Higher Ego has consumed and subjected for ever the passional nature of the personal, lower Ego, is easy, but requires an adept; and (*b*) of being a reincarnation of one, who, in a previous birth, had attained through extreme purity of life and efforts in the right direction almost to a *Yogi*-state of holiness and saintship. There is also a third possibility of reaching in mystic visions the plane .of the higher Manas; but it is only occasional and does not depend on the will of the Seer, but on the extreme weakness' and exhaustion of the material body through illness and suffering. The Seeress of

[1] Another name for the universal mind.

Prevorst was an instance of the latter case; and Jacob Boehme of our second category. In all other cases of abnormal seership, of so-called clairaudience, clairvoyance, and trances, it is simply—*mediumship.*

Now what is a medium? The term medium, when not applied simply to things and objects, is supposed to be a person through whom the action of another person or being is either manifested or transmitted. Spiritualists believing in communications with disembodied spirits, and that these can manifest through, or impress sensitives to transmit "messages" from them, regard mediumhip as a blessing and a great privilege. We Theosophists, on the other hand, who do not believe in the "communion of spirits" as Spiritualists do, regard the gift as one of the most dangerous of abnormal nervous diseases. A medium is simply one in whose personal Ego, or terrestrial mind (*psuche*), the percentage of "astral" light so preponderates as to impregnate with it his whole physical constitution. Every organ and cell thereby is attuned, so to speak, and subjected to an enormous and abnormal tension. The mind is ever on the plane of, and quite immersed in, that deceptive light whose *soul* is divine, but whose body—the light waves on the lower planes—infernal; for they are but the black and disfigured reflections of the earth's memories. The untrained eye of the poor sensitive cannot pierce the dark mist, the dense fog of the terrestrial emanations, to see beyond in the radiant field of the eternal truths. His vision is out of focus. His senses, accustomed from his birth, like those of a native of the London slums, to stench and filth, to the unnatural distortions of sights and images tossed on the kaleidoscopic waves of the astral plane—are unable to discern the true from the false. And thus, the pale, soulless corpses moving in the trackless fields of "Kama-Loka," appear to him the living images of the "dear departed" ones; the broken echoes of once human voices, passing through his mind, suggest to him well co-ordinated phrases, which he repeats, in ignorance that their final form and polish were received in the innermost depths of his own brain factory. And hence the sight and the hearing of that which if seen in its true nature would have struck the medium's heart cold with horror, now fills him with a sense of beatitude and confidence. He really believes that the immeasurable vistas displayed before him are the real spiritual world, the abode of the blessed disembodied angels.

We describe the broad main features and facts of medium-ship, there being no room in such an article for exceptional cases. We maintain—having unfortunately passed at one period of life *personally* through such experiences—that on the whole, mediumship is most dangerous; and *psychic* experiences when accepted indiscriminately lead only to honestly deceiving others, because the medium is the first self-deceived victim. Moreover, a too close association with the "Old Terrestrial Serpent" is infectious. The odic and magnetic currents of the Astral Light often incite to murder, drunkenness, immorality, and, as Éliphas Lévi expresses it, the not altogether pure natures "can be driven- headlong by the blind forces set in motion in the *Light*"—*by* the errors and sins imposed on its waves.

And this is how the great Mage of the XIXth century corroborates the foregoing when speaking of the Astral Light:—

"We have said that 'to acquire magical power, two things are necessary: to disengage the will from all servitude, and to exercise it in control.

The sovereign will (of the adept) is represented in our symbols by the woman who crushes the serpent's head, and by the resplendent angel who represses the dragon, and holds him under his foot and spear; the great magical agent, the dual current of light, the living astral fire of the earth, has been represented in the ancient theogonies by the serpent with the head of a bull, a ram, or a dog. It is the double serpent of the *caduceus,* it is the Old Serpent of *Genesis,* but it is also the *brazen serpent of Moses* entwined around the tau, that is to say, the generative lingam. It is also the goat of the witch-sabbath, and the Baphomet of the Templars; it is the *Hylé* of the Gnostics; it is the double tail of the serpent which forms the legs of the solar cock of Abraxas; finally, it is the Devil of M. Eudes de Mirville. But in very fact it is the blind force which souls (*i.e.,* the lower *Manas* or *Nephesh*) have to conquer to liberate themselves from the bonds of the earth; for if their will does not free 'them from this *fatal attraction,* they will be absorbed in the current by the force which has produced them, and will return to *the central and eternal fire*'''.[1]

The "central and eternal fire" is that disintegrating Force, that gradually consumes and burns out the *Kama Rupa,* or "personality," in the *Kama Loka,* whither it goes after death. And verily, the Mediums are attracted by the astral light, it is the direct cause of their personal "souls" being absorbed "by the force which has produced" their terrestrial elements. And, therefore, as the same Occultist tells us:—

"All the magical operations consist in *freeing* one's self from the coils of the Ancient Serpent; then to place the foot on its head, and lead it according to the operator's will. 'I will give unto thee,' says the Serpent, in the Gospel myth, 'all the kingdoms of the earth, if thou wilt fall down and worship me.' The initiate should reply to him, "I will not fall down, but thou shalt crouch at my feet; thou wilt give me nothing, but I will make use of thee and take whatever I wish. For *I am thy Lord and Master!"*

And as such, the *Personal Ego, becoming* at one with its divine parent, shares in the immortality of the latter. Otherwise. .

Enough, however. Blessed is he who has acquainted himself with the dual powers at work in the ASTRAL LIGHT; thrice blessed he who has learned to discern the *Noetic* from the *Psychic* action of the "Double-Faced" God in him, and who knows the potency of his own Spirit—or "Soul Dynamics."

---

[1] *Dogme et Rituel de la Haute Magie,* quoted in *Isis Unveiled,* I, 138.

STUDIES IN OCCULTISM

A Series of Reprints from the Writings

of

H. P. BLAVATSKY

NO. IV

KOSMIC MIND

THE DUEL ASPECT OF WISDOM

KOSMIC MIND.

"Whatsoever quits the *Laya* (homogeneous) state, becomes active, conscious life. Individual consciousness emanates from, and returns into Absolute consciousness which is eternal MOTION."

(Esoteric Axioms.)

"Whatever that be which thinks, which understands, which wills, which acts, it is something celestial and divine, and upon that account must necessarily be eternal."
—CICERO.

EDISON'S conception of matter was quoted in our March editorial article. The great American electrician is reported by Mr. G. Parsons Lathrop in *Harper's Magazine* as giving out his personal belief about the atoms being "possessed by a certain amount of intelligence", and shown indulging in other reveries of this kind. For this flight of fancy the February *Review of Reviews* takes the inventor of the phonograph to task, and critically remarks that "Edison is much given to dreaming", his 'scientific imagination' being constantly at work.

Would to goodness the men of science exercised their 'scientific imagination' a little more, and their dogmatic and cold negations a little less. Dreams differ. In that strange state of being which, as Byron has it, puts us in a position "with seal'd eyes to see", one often perceives more real facts than when awake. Imagination is, again, one of the strongest elements in human nature, or in the words of Dugald Stewart, it "is the great spring of human activity and the principal source of human improvement. . . . Destroy the faculty, and the condition of men will become as stationary as that of brutes." It is the best guide of our blind senses, without which the latter could never lead us beyond matter and its illusions. The greatest discoveries of modern science are due to the imaginative faculty of the discovers. But when has anything new been postulated, when a theory clashing with and contradicting a comfortably settled predecessor put forth, without orthodox science first sitting on it, and trying to crush it out of existence? Harvey was also regarded at first as a "dreamer" and a madman to boot. Finally, the whole of modern science is formed of "working hypotheses", the fruits of "scientific imagination", as Mr. Tyndall felicitously called it.

Is it then, because consciousness in every universal atom and the possibility of a complete control over the cells and atoms of his body by man, have not been honored so far with the *imprimatur* of the Popes of exact science, that the idea is to be dismissed as a dream? Occultism gives the same teaching. Occultism tells us that every atom, like the monad of Leibnitz, is a little universe in itself; and that every organ and cell in the human body is endowed with a brain of its own, with memory, therefore, experience and discriminative powers. The idea of Universal Life composed of individual atomic lives is one of the oldest teachings of esoteric philosophy, and the very modern hypothesis of modern science, that of *crystalline life,* is the first ray from the ancient luminary of knowledge that has reached our scholars. If plants can be shown to have nerves and sensations and instinct (but another word for consciousness), why not allow the same in the cells of the human body? Science divides matter into organic and inorganic bodies, only because it rejects the idea of *absolute life* and a life-principle as an entity: otherwise it would be the first to see that *absolute life* cannot produce even a geometrical point, or an atom inorganic in its essence. But Occultism, you see, "teaches mysteries", they say; and mystery is the *negation of common sense,* just as again metaphysics is but a kind of poetry, according to Mr. Tyndall. There is no such thing for science as mystery; and therefore, as a life-principle is, and must remain for the intellects of our civilized races forever a mystery *on physical lines*—they who deal in this question have to be of necessity either fools or knaves.

Dixit. Nevertheless, we may repeat with a French preacher: "mystery is the fatality of science". Official science is surrounded on every side and hedged in by unapproachable, for ever impenetrable mysteries. And why? Simply because physical science is self-doomed to a squirrel-like progress around a wheel of matter limited by our five senses. And though it is as confessedly ignorant of the formation of matter, as of the generation of a simple cell; though it is as powerless to explain what is this, that, or the other, it will yet dogmatize and insist on what life, matter, and the rest are not. It comes to this: the words of Father Felix addressed fifty years ago to the French academicians have nearly become immortal as a truism. "Gentlemen", he said, "you throw into our teeth the reproach that we teach mysteries. But imagine whatever science you will; follow the magnificent sweep of its deductions   and when you arrive at its parent source you come face to face with the unknown!"

Now to lay at rest once for all in the minds of theosophists this vexed question, we intend to prove that modern science, owing to physiology, is itself on the eve of discovering that consciousness is universal—thus justifying Edison's "dreams". But before we do this, we mean also to show that though many a man of science is soaked through and through with such belief, very few are brave enough to openly admit it, as the late Dr. Pirogoff of St. Petersburg has done in his posthumous *Memoirs.* Indeed that great surgeon and pathologist raised by their publication quite a howl of indignation among his colleagues. How then? the public asked: He, Dr. Pirogoff, whom we regarded as almost the embodiment of European learning, believing in the superstitions of crazy alchemists? He, who in the words of a contemporary:—

was the very incarnation of exact science and methods of thought; who had dissected hundreds and thousands of human organs, making himself as acquainted with all the mysteries of surgery and anatomy as we are with our familiar furniture; the savant for whom physiology had no secrets and who, above all men, was one to whom Voltaire might have ironically asked whether he had not found immortal soul between the bladder and the blind gut,—that same Pirogoff is found after his death devoting whole chapters in his literary Will to the scientific demonstration. . . . .

Novoye Vremya of 1887.

—of what? Why, of the existence in every organism *of a distinct* 'VITAL FORCE' in-dependent of any physical or chemical process. Like Liebig he accepted the derided and tabooed homogeneity of nature—a life principle—that persecuted and hapless teleology, or the science of the final causes of things, which is as philosophical as it is *unscientific,* if we have to believe imperial and royal academies. His unpardonable sin in the eyes of dogmatic modern science, how-ever, was this: The great anatomist and surgeon had the 'hardihood' to declare in his *Memoirs,* that:—

"We have no cause to reject the possibility of the existence of organisms endowed with such properties that would make of *them—the direct embodiment of the universal mind—a* perfection inaccessible to our own (human) mind, ...because we have no right to maintain that man is the last expression of the divine creative thought."

Such are the chief features of the heresy of one who ranked high among the men of exact science of this age. His *Memoirs* show plainly that not only he believed in universal deity, divine ideation, or the Hermetic 'thought divine', and a vital principle, but taught all this, and tried to demonstrate it scientifically. Thus he argues that Universal Mind needs no physico-chemical, or mechanical brain as an organ of transmission. He even goes so far as to admit it in these suggestive words:—

"Our reason must accept in *all necessity* an infinite and eternal Mind which rules and governs the ocean of life. . . . . *Thought and creative ideation, in full agreement with the laws of unity* and *causation, manifest themselves plainly enough in universal life without the participation of brain-slush. . . .* Directing the forces and elements toward the formation of organisms, this organizing *life-principle* becomes *self-sentient, Self-conscious, racial* or *individual.* Substance, ruled and *directed by the life-principle,* is organised *according* to a *general defined plan into certain* types. . . . ."

He explains this belief by confessing that never, during his long life so full of study, observation, and experiments, could he—

"acquire the conviction, that our brain could be the only organ of thought in the whole universe; that everything in this world, save *that* organ, should be unconditioned and senseless, and that human thought alone should impart to the universe a meaning and a reasonable harmony in its integrity."

And he adds *à propos* of Moleschott's materialism:—

"Howsoever much fish and peas I may eat, never shall I consent to give away my *Ego* into durance vile of a product casually extracted by modern *alchemy* from the urine. If, in our conceptions of the universe it be our fate to fall into illusions, then my 'illusion' has, at least, the advantage of being very consoling. For it shows to me an intelligent universe and the activity of forces working in it harmoniously and intelligently; and that my 'I' is not the product of chemical and histological elements but an *embodiment of a common universal Mind.* The latter, I sense and represent to myself as acting in freewill and consciousness in accordance with the same laws which are traced for the guidance of my own mind, but only exempt from that restraint which trammels our human conscious individuality."

For, as remarks elsewhere this great and philosophic man of Science:—

"*The limitless and the eternal, is not only a postulate of our mind and reason, but also a gigantic fact, in itself.* What would become of our ethical or moral principle were not the everlasting and integral truth to serve it as a foundation!"

The above selections, translated *verbatim* from the confessions of one who was during his long life a star of the first magnitude in the fields of pathology and surgery, show him imbued and soaked through with the philosophy of a reasoned and scientific mysticism. In reading the *Memoirs* of that man of scientific fame, we feel proud of finding him accepting, almost wholesale, the fundamental doctrines and beliefs of Theosophy. With such an exceptionally scientific mind in the ranks of mystics, the idiotic grins, the cheap satires and flings at our great Philosophy by some European and American 'Freethinkers', become almost a compliment. More than ever do they appear to us like the frightened discordant cry of the night-owl hurrying to hide in its dark ruins before the light of the morning Sun.

The progress of physiology itself, as we have just said, is a sure warrant that the dawn of that day when a full recognition of a universally diffused mind will be an accomplished fact, is not far off. It is *only a* question of time.

For, notwithstanding the boast of physiology, that the aim of its researches is only the summing up of every vital function in order to bring them into a definite order by showing their mutual relations to, and connection with, the laws of physics and chemistry, hence, in their final form with mechanical laws—we fear there is a good deal of contradiction between the confessed object and the speculations of some of the best of our modern physiologists. While few of them would dare to return as openly as did Dr. Pirogoff to the 'exploded superstition' of *vitalism* and the severely exiled life-principle, the *principium vitæ* of Paracelsus—yet physiology stands sorely perplexed in the face of its ablest representatives before certain facts. Unfortunately for us, this age of ours is not conducive to the development of moral courage. The time for most to act on the noble idea of *'principia non homines',* has not yet come. And yet there are exceptions to the general rule, and physiology—whose destiny it is to become the hand-maiden of Occult truths—has not let the latter remain without their witnesses. There are those who are already stoutly protesting against certain hitherto favorite propositions. For instance, some physiologists are already denying that it is the forces and substances of so-called 'inanimate' nature, which are acting exclusively in living beings. For, as they well argue:—

"The fact that we reject the interference of other forces in living things, *depends entirely on the limitations of our senses.* We use, indeed, the same organs for our observations of both animate and inanimate nature; and these organs can receive manifestations of only a *limited* realm of motion. Vibrations passed along the fibres of our optic nerves to the brain reach our perceptions through our consciousness as sensations of light and color; vibrations affecting our consciousness through our auditory organs strike us as sounds; all our feelings, through whichever of our senses, are duo to nothing but motions."

Such are the teachings of physical Science, and such were in their roughest outlines those of Occultism, æons and millenniums back. The difference, however, and most vital distinction between the two teachings, is this: official science sees in motion simply a blind, unreasoning force or law; Occultism, tracing motion to its origin, identifies it with the Universal Deity, and calls this eternal ceaseless motion—the 'Great Breath'.[1]

Nevertheless, however limited the conception of modern science about the said Force, still it is suggestive enough to have forced the following remark from a great scientist, the present professor of physiology at the University of Basle,[2] who speaks like an occultist.

"It would be folly in us to expect to be ever able to discover, with the assistance only of our external senses, in animate nature that something which we are unable to find in the inanimate."

And forthwith the lecturer adds that man being endowed "in addition to his physical senses with an *inner sense"*, a perception which gives him the possibility of observing the states and phenomena of his own consciousness, "he has to use *that* in dealing with animate nature"—a profession of faith verging suspiciously on

---

[1] *Vide Secret Doctrine, vol.* i, pp. 2 and 3.
[2] From a paper read by him some time ago at a public lecture.

the borders of Occultism. He denies, moreover, the assumption, that the states and phenomena of consciousness represent in substance the same manifestations of motion as in the external world, and bases his denial by the reminder that not all of such states and manifestations have necessarily a spatial extension. According to him that only is connected with our conception of space which has reached our consciousness through sight, touch, and the muscular sense, while all the other senses, all the *affects,* tendencies, as all the interminable series of representations, have no extension in space but only in time.

Thus he asks:—

"Where then is there room in this for a mechanical theory? Objectors might argue that this is so only in appearance, while in reality all these have a spatial extension. But such an argument would be entirely erroneous. Our sole reason for believing that objects perceived by the senses have such extension in the external world, rests on the idea that they seem to do so, as far as they can be watched and observed through the senses of sight and touch. With regard, however, to the realm of our *inner* senses even that supposed foundation loses its force and there is no ground for admitting it."

The winding up argument of the lecturer is most interesting to theosophists. Says this physiologist of the modern school of Materialism:—

"Thus, a deeper and more direct acquaintance with *our inner nature* unveils to us a world *entirely unlike the world represented to us by our external senses,* and reveals the most heterogeneous faculties, shows objects having naught to do with spatial extension, and phenomena absolutely disconnected with those that fall under mechanical laws."

Hitherto, the opponents of vitalism and 'life-principle', as well as the followers of the mechanical theory of life, based their views on the supposed fact, that, as physiology was progressing forward, its students succeeded more and more in connecting its functions with the laws of *blind matter.* All those manifestations that used to be attributed to a 'mystical life-force', they said, may be brought now under physical and chemical laws. And they were, and still are loudly clamoring for the recognition of the fact that it is only a question of time when it will be triumphantly demonstrated that the whole vital process, in its grand totality, represents nothing more mysterious than a very complicated phenomenon of motion, exclusively governed by the forces of inanimate nature.

But here we have a professor of physiology who asserts that the history of physiology proves, unfortunately for them, quite the contrary; and he pronounces these ominous words:—

"I maintain that the more our experiments and observations are exact and many-sided, the deeper we penetrate into facts, the more we try to fathom and speculate on the phenomena of life, the more we acquire the conviction that even those phenomena that we had hoped to be already able to explain by physical and chemical laws, *are in reality unfathomable.* They are vastly more complicated, in fact; and as we stand at present, *they will not yield to any mechanical explanation."*

This is a terrible blow at the puffed-up bladder known as Materialism, which is as empty as it is dilated. A Judas in the camp of the apostles of negation—the 'animalists'! But the Basle professor is no solitary exception, as we have just shown; and there are several physiologists who are of his way of thinking; indeed some of them going so far as to almost accept *free-will* and *consciousness,* in the simplest monadic protoplasms!

One discovery after the other tends in this direction. The works of some German physiologists are especially interesting with regard to cases of consciousness and positive discrimination—one is almost inclined to say *thought*—in the *Amœbœ*. Now the Amoebae or animalculæ are, as all know, microscopical protoplasms—as the *Vampyrella Spirogyra* for instance, a most simple elementary cell, a protoplasmic drop, formless and almost structureless. And yet it shows in its behavior something for which zoologists, if they do not call it mind and power of reasoning, will have to find some other qualification, and coin a new term. For see what Cienkowsky[1] says of it. Speaking of this microscopical, bare, reddish cell he describes the way in which it hunts for and finds among a number of other aquatic plants one called *Spirogyra*, rejecting every other food. Examining its perigrinations under a powerful microscope, he found it when moved by hunger, first projecting its *pseudopodiœ* (false feet) by the help of which it crawls. Then it commences moving about until among a great variety of plants it comes across a *Spirogyra*, after which it proceeds toward the cellulated portion of one of the cells of the latter, and placing itself on it, it bursts the tissue, sucks the contents of one cell and then passes on to another, repeating the same process. This naturalist never saw it take any other food, and it never touched any of the numerous plants placed by Cienkowsky in its way. Mentioning another Amœba—the *Colpadella Pugnax*—he says that he found it showing the same predilection for the *Chlamydomonas* on which it feeds exclusively; "having made a puncture in the body of the Chlamydomonas it sucks its chlorophyl and then goes away", he writes, adding these significant words: "The way of acting of these monads during their search for and reception of food, is so amazing that one is almost inclined to see in them *consciously acting beings!"*

Not less suggestive are the observations of Th. W. Engelman *(Beiträge zur Physiologie des Protoplasm),* on the *Arcella,* another unicellular organism only a trifle more complex than the *Vampyrella.* He shows them in a drop of water under a microscope on a piece of glass, lying so to speak, on their backs, *i.e.,* on their convex side, so that the *pseudopodiœ,* projected from the edge of the shell, find no hold in space and leave the Amœba helpless. Under these circumstances the following curious fact is observed. Under the very edge of one of the sides of the protoplasm gas-bubbles begin immediately to form, which, making that side lighter, allow it to be raised, bringing at the same time the opposite side of the creature into contact with the glass, thus furnishing its *pseudo* or false feet means to get hold of the surface and thereby turning over its body to raise itself on all its *pseudopodiœ.* After this, the Amœba proceeds to suck back into itself the gas bubbles and begins to move. If a like drop of water is placed on the lower extremity of the glass, then following the law of gravity the Amœbae will find themselves at first at the lower end of the drop of water. Failing to find there a point of support, they proceed to generate large bubbles of gas, when, becoming lighter than the water, they are raised up to the surface of the drop.

In the words of Engelman:—

"If having reached the surface of the glass they find no more support for their feet than before, forthwith one sees the gas-globules diminishing on one side and increasing in size and number on the other, or both, until the creatures touch with the edge of their shell the

---

[1] L. Cienkowsky. See his work *Betträge zur Kentniss der Monaden,* Archiv. f. mikroskop, Anatomie.

surface of the glass, and are enabled to turn over. No sooner is this done than the glass-globules disappear and the *Arcelæ* begin crawling. Detach them carefully by means of a fine needle from the surface of the glass and thus bring them down once more to the lower surface of the drop of water; and forwith they will repeat the same process, varying its details according to necessity and devising new means to reach their desired aim. Try as much as you will to place them in uncomfortable positions, and they find means to extricate themselves from them, each time, by one device or the other; and no sooner have they succeeded than the gas-bubbles disappear I It is impossible not to admit that such facts as these point *to the presence of some* PSYCHIC *process in the protoplasm."* [1]

Among hundreds of accusations against Asiatic nations of degrading *super-stitions,* based on 'crass ignorance', there exists no more serious denunciation than that which accuses and convicts them of personifying and *even deifying* the chief organs *of,* and in, the human body. Indeed, do not we hear these 'benighted fools' of Hindus speaking of the small-pox as a goddess—thus personifying the microbes of the variolic virus? Do we not read about *Tantrikas,* a sect of mystics, giving proper names to nerves, cells and arteries, connecting and identifying various parts of the body with deities, endowing functions and physiological processes with intelligence, and what not? The vertebræ, fibres, ganglia, the cord, etc., of the spinal column; the heart, its four chambers, auricle and ventricle, valves and the rest; stomach, liver, lungs, and spleen, everything has its special deific name, is believed *to act consciously* and to act under the potent will of the Yogi, whose head and heart are the seats of Brahmâ and the various parts of whose body are all the pleasure grounds of this or another deity

This is indeed *ignorance.* Especially when we think that the said organs, and the whole body of man are composed of cells, and these cells are now being recognized as individual organisms and—*quien sabe*—*will* come perhaps to be recognized some day as *an independent race of thinkers* inhabiting the globe, called man! It really looks like it. For was it not hitherto believed that all the phenomena of assimilation and sucking in of food by the intestinal canal, could be explained by the laws of diffusion and endosmosis? And now, alas, physiologists have come to learn that the action of the intestinal canal during the act of absorbing, is not identical with the action of the non-living membrane in the dialyser. It is now well demonstrated that—

"this wall is covered with epithelium cells, each of which is an organism *per se,* a living being, and with very complex functions. We know further, that such a cell assimilates food—by means of active contractions of its protoplasmic body—in a manner as mysterious as that which we notice in the independent Amœbæ and animalculæ. We can observe on the intestinal epithelium of the cold-blooded animals how these cells project shoots—*pseudopodiæ*—out of their contractive, bare, protoplasmic bodies—which *pseudopodiæ,* or false feet, fish out of the food drops of fat, suck them into their protoplasm and send it further, toward the lymph-duct. . . . The lymphatic cells issuing from the nests of the adipose tissue, and squeezing themselves through the epithelium cells up to the surface of the intestines, absorb therein the drops of fat and loaded with their prey, travel homeward to the lymphatic canals. So long as this active work of the cells remained unknown to us, the fact that while the globules of fat penetrated through the walls of the intestines into lymphatic channels, the smallest of pigmental grains introduced into the intestines did not do so,— remained unexplained. But today we know, that this faculty of selecting their special food—

---

[1] *Loc. cit.,* Pflüger's Archiv. Bd. II, S. 387.

of assimilating the useful and rejecting the useless and the harmful—is common to all the unicellular organisms."[1]

And the lecturer queries, why, if this *discrimination* in the selection of food exists in the simplest and most elementary of the cells, in the formless and structureless protoplasmic *drops*—why it should not exist also in the epithelium cells of our intestinal canal. Indeed, if the *Vampyrella* recognizes its much beloved *Spirogyra,* among hundreds of other plants as shown above, why should not the epithelium cell, *sense, choose* and *select* its favorite drop of fat from a pigmental grain? But we will be told that 'sensing, choosing and selecting' pertain only to reasoning beings, at least to the *instinct* of more structural animals than is the protoplasmic cell outside or inside man. Agreed; but as we translate from the lecture of a learned physiologist and the works of other learned naturalists, we can only say, that these learned gentlemen must know what they are talking about; though they are probably ignorant of the fact that their *scientific* prose is but one degree removed from the *ignorant, superstitious,* but rather poetical 'twaddle' of the Hindu Yogis and Tantrikas.

Anyhow, our professor of physiology falls foul of the materialistic theories of diffusion and endosmosis. Armed with the facts of the evident discrimination and a *mind* in the cells, he demonstrates by numerous instances the fallacy of trying to explain certain physiological processes by mechanical theories; such for instance as the passing of sugar from the liver (where it is transformed into glucose) into the blood. Physiologists find great difficulty in explaining this process, and *regard it as an impossibility to bring it under the endosmosic laws.* In all probability the lymphatic cells play just as active a part during the absorption of alimentary substances dissolved in water, as the peptics do, a process well demonstrated by F. Hofmeister.[2] Generally speaking, poor convenient endosmose is dethroned and exiled from among the active functionaries of the human body as a useless sinecurist. It has lost its voice in the matter of glands and other agents of secretion, in the action of which the same epithelium cells have replaced it. The mysterious faculties of selection, of extracting from the blood one kind of substance and rejecting another, of transforming the former by means of decomposition and synthesis, of directing some of the products into passages which will throw them out of the body and redirecting others into the lymphatic and blood vessels—such is the work of the cells. *"It is evident that in all this there is not the slightest hint at diffusion or endosmose",* says the Basle physiologist. *"It becomes entirely useless to try and explain these phenomena by chemical laws."*

But perhaps physiology is luckier in some other department? Failing in the laws of alimentation it may have found some consolation for its mechanical theories in the question of the activity of muscles and nerves, which it sought to explain by electric laws? Alas, save in a few fishes—in no other living organisms, least of all in the human body, could it find any possibility of pointing out electric currents as the chief ruling agency. Electro-biology on the lines of pure dynamic electricity has egregiously failed. Ignorant of 'Fohat' no electrical currents suffice to explain to it either muscular or nervous activity!

---

[1] From the paper read by the Professor of Physiology at the University of Basle, previously quoted.

[2] *Untersuchungen liber Resorption u. Assimilation der Nährstoffe* (Archiv f. Experimentalle Pathologie und Pharmakologie, Bd. XIX, 1885).

But there is such a thing as the physiology of external sensations. Here we are no longer on *terra incognita,* and all such phenomena have already found purely *physical* explanations. No doubt there is the phenomenon of sight, the eye with its optical apparatus, its camera obscura. But the fact of the sameness of the reproduction of things in the eye, according to the same laws of refraction as on the plate of a photographic machine, is *no vital phenomenon.* The same may be reproduced *on a dead eye.* The phenomenon of life consists *in the evolution and development of the eye itself.* How is this marvellous and complicated work produced? To this physiology replies, "We do not know"; for, toward the solution of this great problem—

"Physiology has not yet made one single step. True, we can follow the sequence of the stages of the development and formation of the eye, but *why* it is so and *what* is the causal connection, we have absolutely no idea. The second vital phenomenon of the eye is its accommodating activity. And here we are again face to face with the functions of nerves and muscles—our old insoluble riddles. The same may be said of all the organs of sense. The same also relates to other departments of physiology. We had hoped to explain the phenomena of the circulation of the blood by the laws of hydrostatics or hydrodynamics. Of course the blood moves in accordance with the hydrodynamical laws; but its relation to them remains utterly *passive.* As to the *active* functions of the heart and the muscles of its vessels, *no one, so* far, has ever *been able to explain them by physical laws.*"

The underlined words in the concluding portion of the able Professor's lecture are worthy of an Occultist. Indeed, he seems to be repeating an aphorism from the "Elementary Instructions" of the esoteric physiology of *practical* Occultism:—

"*The riddle of life is found in the active functions of a living organsim,*[1] *the real perception of which activity we can get only through self-observation, and not owing to our external senses;* by observation on our will, so far as it penetrates our consciousness, thus revealing itself to our inner sense. Therefore, when the same phenomenon acts only on our external senses, we recognize it no longer. We see everything that takes place around and near the phenomenon of motion, but the essence of that phenomenon we do not see at all, because we lack for it a special organ of receptivity. We can accept that *ease in* a mere hypothetical way, and do so, in fact, when we speak of 'active functions'. Thus does every physiologist, for he cannot go on without such hypothesis; and this is a first experiment of a *psychological explanation* of all vital phenomena. . . . . And if it is demonstrated to us that we are unable with the help only of physics and chemistry to explain the phenomena of life, what may we expect from other adjuncts of physiology, from the sciences of morphology, anatomy, and histology? I maintain that these can never help us to unriddle the problem of any of the mysterious phenomena of life. For after we have succeeded with the help of scalpel and microscope in dividing the organisms into their most elementary compounds, and reached the simplest of cells, it is just here that we find ourselves face to face with the greatest problem of all. The simplest monad, a microscopical point of protoplasm, formless and structureless, exhibits yet all the essential vital functions, alimentation, growth, breeding, motion, feeling and sensuous perception, and even such functions which replace 'consciousness'—the soul of the higher animals!"

The problem—for materialism—is a terrible one, indeed! Shall our cells, and

---

[1] *Life* and *activity* are but the two different names for the same idea, or, what is still more correct, they are two words with which the men of science connect no definite idea whatever. Nevertheless, and perhaps just for that, they are obliged to use them, for they contain the point of contact between the most difficult problems over which, in fact, the greatest thinkers of the materialistic school have ever tripped.

infinitesimal monads in nature, do for us that which the arguments of the greatest Pantheistic philosophers have hitherto failed to do? Let us hope so. And if they do, then the superstitious and ignorant' Eastern Yogis, and even their exoteric followers, will find themselves vindicated. For we hear from the same physiologist that—

"A large number of poisons are prevented by the epithelium *cells* from penetrating into lymphatic spaces, though we know that they are easily decomposed in the abdominal and intestinal juices. More than this. Physiology is aware that by injecting these poisons directly into the blood, they will separate from, and reappear through the intestinal walls, and that in this process the *lymphatic cells* take a most active part."

If the reader turns to *Webster's Dictionary* he will find therein a curious explanation at the words "lymphatic" and "lymph". Etymologists think that the Latin word *lympha* is derived from the Greek *nymphe*, *"a* nymph or *inferior Goddess"*, they say. "The Muses were some. times called *nymphs* by the poets. Hence (according to Webster) all persons in a state of rapture, as seers, poets, madmen, etc., were said to be caught by the nymphs (νυμφόληπτοι)."

The Goddess of Moisture (the Greek and Latin *nymph* or *lymph,* then) is fabled in India as being born from the *pores* of one of the Gods, whether the Ocean God, Varuna, or a minor River God' is left to the particular sect and fancy of the believers. But the main question is, that the ancient Greeks and Latins are thus admittedly known to have shared in the same 'superstitions' as the Hindus. This superstition is shown in their maintaining to this day that every atom of matter in the four (or five) Elements is an emanation from an inferior God or Goddess, himself or herself an earlier emanation from a superior deity; and, moreover, that each of these atoms—being Brahmâ, one of whose names is *Anu,* or atom—no sooner is it emanated than it *becomes endowed with consciousness,* each of its kind, and free-will, acting within the limits of law. Now, he who knows that the *kosmic trimurti* (trinity) composed of Brahmâ, the Creator; Vishnu, the Preserver; and Siva, the Destroyer, is *a* most magnificent and scientific symbol of the *material* Universe and its gradual evolution; and who finds a proof of this, in the etymology of the names of these deities,[1] *plus* the doctrines of *Gupta Vidya,* or esoteric knowledge—knows also how to correctly understand this 'superstition'. The five fundamental titles of Vishnu—added to that of *Anu* (atom), common to all the trimurtic personages—which are, *Bhutâtman,* one with the created or emanated materials of the world; *Pradhanâtman,* 'one with the senses'; *Paramâtman,* 'Supreme Soul'; and *Atman,* Kosmic Soul, or the Universal Mind— show sufficiently what the ancient Hindus meant by endowing with mind and consciousness every atom and giving it a distinct name of a God or a Goddess. Place their Pantheon, composed of 30 crores (or 300 millions) of deities within the macrocosm (the Universe), or inside the microcosm (man), and the number will not be found overrated, since they relate to the atoms, cells, and molecules of everything that is.

This, no doubt, is too poetical and abstruse for our generation, but it seems decidedly as scientific, if not more so, than the teachings derived from the latest

---

[1] *Brahmâ* comes from the root *brih*, 'to expand' to 'scatter'; *Vishnu* from the root vis or vish (phonetically) 'to enter into', 'to pervade' the universe, of matter. As to Siva—the patron of the Yogis, the etymology of his name would remain *incomprehensible to* the casual reader.

discoveries of *Physiology* and *Natural History*.

THE DUAL ASPECT OF WISDOM.

"No doubt but ye are the people and wisdom shall die with you."
Jon xii. 2.

"But wisdom is justified of her children."
MATTHEW xi. 19.

IT is the privilege—as also occasionally the curse—of editors to receive numerous letters of advice, and the conductors of LUCIFER have not escaped the common lot. Reared in the aphorisms of the ages they are aware that "he who can take advice is superior to him who gives it", and are therefore ready to accept with gratitude any sound and practical suggestions offered by friends; but the last letter received does not fulfill the condition. It is not even his own wisdom, but that of the age we live in, which is asserted by our adviser, who thus seriously risks his reputation for keen observation by such acts of devotion on the altar of modern pretensions. It is in defence of the 'wisdom' of our century that we are taken to task, and charged with "preferring barbarous antiquity to our modern civilization and its inestimable boons", with forgetting that "our own-day wisdom compared with the awakening instincts of the Past is in no way inferior in *philosophic wisdom* even to the age of Plato". We are lastly told that we, theosophists, are "too fond of the dim yesterday, and as unjust to our glorious (?) present-day, the bright noon-hour of the highest civilization and culture"!!

Well, all this is a question of taste. Our correspondent is welcome to his own views, but so are we to ours. Let him imagine that the Eiffel Tower dwarfs the Pyramid of Ghizeh into a mole-hill, and the Crystal Palace grounds transform the hanging gardens of Semiramis into a kitchen-garden—if he likes. But if we are seriously 'challenged' by him to show "in what respect our age of hourly progress and gigantic thought"—a progress a trifle marred, however, by our Huzleys being denounced by our Spurgeons, and the University ladies, senior classics and wranglers, by the 'hallelujah lasses'—is inferior to the ages of, say, a hen-pecked "Socrates and a cross-legged Buddha", then we will answer him, giving him, of course, our own personal opinion.

Our age, we say, is inferior in wisdom to any other, because it professes, more visibly every day, *contempt for truth and justice, without which there can be no wisdom.* Because our civilization, built up of shams and appearances, is at best like a beautiful green morass, a bog, spread over a deadly quagmire. Because this century of culture and worship of matter, while offering prizes and premiums for every *best* thing' under the sun, from the biggest baby and the largest orchid down to the strongest pugilist and the fattest pig, has no encouragement to offer to morality; no prize to give for any moral virtue. Because it has societies for the prevention of physical cruelty to animals, and none with the object of preventing the moral cruelty practiced on human beings. Because it encourages, legally and tacitly, vice under every form, from the sale of whisky down to forced prostitution and theft brought on by starvation wages, Shylock-like exactions, rents, and other comforts of our cultured period. Because, finally, this is the age which, although proclaimed as one of physical and moral freedom, is in truth the age of the most ferocious moral and mental slavery, the like of which was never known before. Slavery to State and *men* has disappeared only to make room for slavery to *things* and *Self,* to one's own vices and idiotic social customs and ways. Rapid civilization, adapted to the needs of the higher and middle classes, has doomed by

71

contrast to only greater wretchedness the starving masses. Having levelled the two former it has made them the more to disregard the substance in favor of form and appearance, thus forcing modern man into duress vile, a slavish dependence on things inanimate, to use and to serve which is the first bounden duty of every *cultured* man.

Where then is the Wisdom of our modern age?

In truth, it requires but a very few lines to show why we bow before ancient Wisdom, while refusing absolutely to see any in our modern civilization. But to begin with, what does our critic mean by the word 'wisdom'? Though we have never too unreasonably admired Lactantius, yet we must recognize that even that innocent Church Father, with all his cutting insults anent the heliocentric system, defined the term very correctly when saying that "the first point of Wisdom is to discern that which is false, and the second, to know that which is true". And if so, what chance is there for our century of falsification, from the revised Bible texts down to natural butter, to put forth a claim to Wisdom'? But before we cross lances on this subject we may do well, perchance, to define the term ourselves.

Let us premise by saying that Wisdom is, at best, an elastic word—at any rate as used in European tongues. That it yields no clear idea of its meaning, unless preceded or followed by some qualifying adjective. In the Bible, indeed, the Hebrew equivalent *Chokmah* (in Greek, *Sophia*) is applied to the most dissimilar things—abstract and concrete. Thus we find 'Wisdom' as the characteristic both of divine inspiration and also of terrestrial cunning and craft ; as meaning the Secret Knowledge of the Esoteric Sciences, and also blind faith; the "fear of the Lord", and Pharaoh's magicians. The noun is indifferently applied to Christ and to sorcery, for the witch Sedecla is also referred to as the *"wise woman of En-Dor"*. From the earliest Christian antiquity, beginning with St. James (iii, 13-17), down to the last Calvinist preacher, who sees in hell and eternal damnation a proof of "the Almighty's *wisdom"*, the term has been used with the most varied meanings. But St. James teaches two kinds of wisdom; a teaching with which we fully concur. He draws a strong line of separation between the divine or *noëtic* 'Sophia'—the Wisdom from above—and the terrestrial, psychic, and devilish wisdom—the Sophia ἐπίγειος, ψυχική, δαιμονιώδης (iii, 15). For the true theoso-phist there is no wisdom save the former. Would that such an one could declare with Paul, that he speaks that wisdom exclusively only among them "that are perfect", *i.e.,* those initiated into its mysteries, or familiar, at least, with the A B C of the sacred sciences. But, however great was his mistake, however premature his attempt to sow the seeds of the *true and eternal gnosis* on unprepared soil, his motives were yet good and his intention unselfish, and *therefore* has he been stoned. For had he only attempted to preach some particular fiction of his own, or done it for gain, who would have ever singled him out or tried to crush him, amid the hundreds of other false sects, daily 'collections' and crazy 'societies'? But his case was different. However cautiously, still he spoke "not the wisdom of this world" but *truth* or the "hidden wisdom . . . . which none of the Princes of this world know" (1 Corinth. ii.) least of all the *archons* of our modern science. With regard to 'psychic' wisdom, however, which James defines as terrestrial and devilish, it has existed in all ages, from the days of Pythagoras and Plato, when for one *philosophus* there were nine *sophistæ,* down to our modern era. To such wisdom our century is welcome, and indeed fully entitled, to lay a claim. Moreover, it is an attire easy to put on; there never was a period when crows refused to array themselves in peacocks' feathers, if the opportunity was offered.

But now as then, we have a right to analyze the terms used and enquire in the words of the book of Job, that suggestive allegory of Karmic purification and initiatory rites: "Where shall (true) wisdom be found? where is the place of understanding?" and to answer again in his words: "With the ancient *is* wisdom and in the length of days understanding" (Job xxviii, 12, and xii, 12).

Here we have to qualify once more a dubious term, viz: the word 'ancient', and to explain it. As interpreted by the orthodox churches, it has in the mouth of Job one meaning; but with the Kabalist, quite another; while in the Gnosis of the Occultist and Theosophist it has distinctly a third signification, the same which it had in the original *Book of Job,* a pre-Mosaic work and a recognized treatise on Initiation. Thus, the kabalist applies the adjective 'ancient' to the manifested Woltz, on Loops *(Dabar)* of the forever concealed and ancognizable deity. Daniel, in one of his visions, also uses it when speaking of Jahve—the androgynous Adam Kadmon. The Churchman connects it with his anthropomorphic Jehovah, the 'Lord God' of the *translated* Bible. But the Eastern Occultist employs the mystic term only when referring to the re-incarnating higher Ego. For, divine Wisdom being diffused throughout the infinite Universe, and our impersonal HIGHER SELF being an integral part of it, the *atmic* light of the latter can be centered only in that which though eternal is still individualized—*i.e.* the noëtic Principle, the manifested God within each rational being, or our Higher *Mans* at one with *Buddhi.* It is this collective light which is the "Wisdom that is from above", and which whenever it descends on the personal Ego, is found "pure, peaceable, gentle". Hence, Job's assertion that "Wisdom is with the Ancient", or *Buddhi-Manas.* For the Divine Spiritual 'I', is alone eternal, and the same throughout all births; whereas the personalities' it informs in succession are evanescent, changing like the shadows of a kaleidoscopic series of forms in a magic lantern. It is the 'Ancient', because, whether it be called Sophia, Krishna, Buddhi-Manas, or Christos, it is ever the 'first-born' of *Alaya-Mahat,* the Universal Soul and the Intelligence of the Universe. Esoterically then, Job's statement must read: "With the Ancient (Man's Higher Ego) *is* Wisdom, and in the length of *days* (or the number of its re-incarnations) is understanding". No man can learn true and final wisdom in one birth; and every new rebirth, whether we be re-incarnated for weal or for woe, is one more lesson we receive at the bands of the stern yet ever just schoolmaster—KARMIC LIFE.

But the world—the Western world, at any rate—knows nothing of this, and refuses to learn anything. For it, any notion of the Divine Ego or the plurality of its births is "heathen foolishness". The Western world rejects these truths, and will recognize no *wise* men except those of its own making, created in its own image, born within its own Christian era and teachings. The only 'wisdom' it understands and practises is the psychic, the "terrestrial and devilish" wisdom spoken of by James, thus making of the *real* Wisdom a misnomer and a degredation. Yet., without considering her multiplied varieties, there are two kinds of even 'terrestrial' wisdom on our globe of mud—the real and the apparent. Between the two, there is even for the superficial observer of this busy, wicked world, a wide chasm, and yet how very few people will consent to see it! The reason for this is quite natural. So strong is human selfishness, that wherever there is the slightest personal interest at stake, there men become deaf and blind to the truth, as often consciously as not. Nor are many people capable of recognizing as speedily as is advisable the difference between men who are wise and those who only *seem* wise, the latter being chiefly regarded as such because they are very clever at blowing their own trumpet. So much for 'wisdom' in the profane world.

As to the world of the students in mystic lore, it is almost worse.Things have strangely altered since the days of antiquity, when the truly wise made it their first duty to conceal their knowledge, deeming it too sacred to even mention before the *hoi polloi.* While the mediæval *Rosecroix,* the true philosopher, keeping old Socrates in mind, repeated daily that all he knew was that he knew nothing, his modern self-styled successor announces in our day, through press and public, that those mysteries in Nature and her occult laws of which he knows nothing, have never existed at all. There was a time when the acquirement of Divine Wisdom *(Sapientia)* required the sacrifice and devotion of a man's whole life. It depended on such things as the purity of the candidate's motives, on his fearlessness and independence of spirit; but now, to receive a patent for wisdom and adeptship requires only unblushing impudence. A certificate of divine wisdom is now decreed and delivered to a self-styled *"Adeptus"* by a regular majority of votes of profane and easily-caught gulls, while a host of magpies driven away from the roof of the Temple of Science will herald it to the world in every market-place and fair. Tell the public that now, even as of old, the genuine and sincere observer of life and its underlying phenomena, the intelligent coworker with nature, may, by becoming an expert in her mysteries thereby become a 'wise' man, in the terrestrial sense of the word, but that never will a *materialist* wrench from nature any secret on a higher plane—and you will be laughed to scorn. Add, that no "wisdom from above" descends on any one save on the *sine quâ non* condition of leaving at the threshold of the occult every atom of selfishness, or desire for personal ends and benefit—and you will be speedily declared by your audience a candidate for the lunatic asylum. Nevertheless, this is an old, very old truism. Nature gives up her innermost secrets and imparts *true wisdom* only to him, who seeks truth for its own sake, and who craves for knowledge in order to confer benefits on others, not on his own unimportant personality. And, as it is precisely to this *personal benefit* that nearly every candidate for adeptship and magic looks, and that few are they, who consent to learn at such a heavy price and so small a benefit for themselves in prospect—the really wise occultists become with every century fewer and rarer. How many are there, in-deed, who would not prefer the will-o'-the-wisp of even passing fame to the steady and ever-growing light of eternal, *divine* knowledge, if the latter has to remain, for all but oneself—a light under a bushel?

The same is the case in the world of materialistic science, where we see a great paucity of really learned men and a host of skin-deep scientists, who yet demand each and all to be regarded as Archimedes and Newtons. As above so below. Scholars who pursue knowledge for the sake of truth and fact, and give these out, however unpalatable, and not for the dubious glory of enforcing on the world their respective personal hobbies—may be counted on the fingers of one hand; while legion is the name of the pretenders. In our day, reputations for learning seem to be built by suggestion on the hypnotic principle, rather than by real merit. The masses cower before him who imposes himself upon them; hence such a galaxy of men regarded as eminent in science, arts, and literature; and if they are so easily accepted, it is precisely because of the gigantic self-opinionatedness and self-assertion of, at any rate, the majority of them. Once thoroughly analyzed, however, how many of such would remain who truly deserve the application of 'wise' even in terrestrial wisdom? How many, we ask, of the so-called authorities' and 'leaders of men' prove much better than those of whom it was said—by one 'wise' indeed—"they be blind leaders of the blind"? That the teachings of neither our modern teachers nor preachers are "wisdom from above" is fully demonstrated. It is proved not by any personal incorrectness in their statements or mistakes in life, for to "err is but human", but by incontrovertible *facts, Wisdom* and *Truth* are synonymous terms, and that which is false or pernicious cannot be *wise*. Therefore, if it is true, as we are told by a well-known representative of the Church of England, that the *Sermon on the Mount* would, in its practical application, mean utter ruin for his country in less than three weeks; and if it is no less true, as asserted by a literary critic of science, that "the knell of Charles Darwinism is rung in Mr. A. R. Wallace's present book",[1] an event already predicted by Quatrefages—then we are left to choose between two courses. We have either to take both Theology and Science on blind faith and trust, or, to proclaim both untrue and untrustworthy. There is, however, a third course open: to *pretend that we believe in both at the same time,* and say nothing, as many do; but this would be sinning against Theosophy and pandering to the prejudices of society—and that we refuse to do. More than this: we declare openly, *quand même,* that not one of the two, neither theologist nor scientist, has the right in the face of this to claim, the one that he preaches that which is divine inspiration, and the other—exact science; since the former enforces that which is, on his own recognition, pernicious to men and states—*i.e.,* the ethics of Christ; and the other (in the person of the eminent naturalist, Mr. A. R. Wallace, as shown by Mr. Samuel Butler) teaches Darwinian evolution, in which he believes no longer; a scheme, moreover, *which has never existed in nature,* if the opponents of Darwinism are correct.

Nevertheless, if anyone would presume to call 'unwise' or 'false' the world-chosen authorities, or declare their respective policies dishonest, he would find himself promptly reduced to silence. To doubt the exalted wisdom of the religion of the late Cardinal Newman, or of the Church of England, or again of our great modern scientists, is to sin against the Holy Ghost and Culture. Woe unto him who refuses to recognize the world's 'Elect'. He has to bow before one or the other, though, if one *is* true, the other *must* be false; and if the 'wisdom' of neither Bishop nor Scientist is "from above"—which is pretty fairly demonstrated by this time—then their 'wisdom' is at best "terrestrial, psychic, devilish".

Now, our readers have to bear in mind that naught of the above is meant as a sign of disrespect for the *true* teachings of Christ, or *true* Science; nor do we judge personalities, but only the systems of our civilized world. Valuing freedom of thought above all things, as the only way of reaching at some future time that Wisdom, of which every theosophist ought to be enamored, we recognize the right to the same freedom in our foes as in our friends. All we contend for is their claim to Wisdom—as we understand this term. Nor do we blame, but rather pity, in our innermost heart, the "wise men" of our age for trying to carry out the only policy

---

[1] See *The Deadlock of Darwinian,* by Samuel Butler, in the *Universal Review* for April, 1890.

that will keep them on the pinnacle of their 'authority'; as they could not, even if they would, act otherwise and preserve their *prestige* with the masses, or escape from being speedily outcasted by their colleagues. The party spirit is so strong with regard to the old tracks and ruts, that to turn on a side path means deliberate treachery to it. Thus, to be regarded now-a-days as an authority in some particular subject, the scientist has to reject *nolens volens* the metaphysical, and the theologian to show contempt for the materialistic teachings. All this is worldly policy and practical common sense, but it is not the *Wisdom* of either Job or James.

Shall it be then regarded as too far fetched, if, basing our words on a life-long observation and experience, we venture to offer our ideas as to the quickest and most efficient means of obtaining our present world's universal respect and becoming an 'authority'? Show the tenderest regard for the corns of every party's hobbies, and offer yourself as the chief executioner, the hangman, of the reputations of men and things regarded as unpopular. Learn, that the great secret of power consists in the art of pandering to popular prejudices, to the World's likes and dislikes. Once this principal condition complied with, he who practices it is certain of attracting to himself the educated and their satellites—the less educated—they whose rule it is to place themselves invariably on the safe side of public opinion. This will lead to a perfect harmony of simultaneous action. For, while the favorite attitude of the cultured is to hide behind the intellectual bulwarks of the favorite leaders of scientific thought, and, *jurare in verba magistri,* that of the less cultured is to transform themselves into the faithful, mechanical telephones of their superiors, and to repeat, like well-trained parrots the *dicta* of their immediate leaders. The now aphoristical precept of Mr. Artemus Ward, the showman of famous memory—"Scratch my back, Mr. Editor, and I will scratch yours"—proves immortally true. The "rising Star", whether he be a theologian, a politician, an author, a scientist, or a journalist—has to begin by scratching the back of public tastes and prejudices—a hypnotic method as old as human vanity. Gradually the hypnotized masses begin to purr, they are ready for 'suggestion'. Suggest whatever you want them to believe, and forthwith they will begin to return your caresses, and purr now to your hobbies, and pander in their turn to anything suggested by theologian, politician, author, scientist or journalist. Such is the simple secret of blossoming into an 'authority' or a 'leader of men'; and such is the secret of our modern-day wisdom.

And this is also the 'secret' and the true reason of the *unpopularity* of LUCIFER and of the ostracism practiced by this same modern world on the Theosophical Society; for neither LUCIFER nor the Society it belongs to has ever followed Mr. Artemus Ward's golden precept. No true Theosophist, in fact, would consent to become the fetish of a fashionable doctrine, any more than he would make himself the slave of a decaying dead-letter system, the spirit from which has disappeared for ever. Neither would he pander to anyone or anything, and therefore would always decline to show belief in that in which he does not, nor can he believe, which is lying to his own soul. Therefore there, where others see "the beauty and graces of modern culture", the Theosophist sees only moral ugliness and the somersaults of the clowns of the so-called cultured centers. For him nothing applies better to modern fashionable society than Sydney Smith's description of Popish ritualism: "Posture and imposture, flections and genuflections, bowing to

76

the right, courtesying to the left, and an immense amount of male (and especially female) millinery". There may be, no doubt, for some worldly minds, a great charm in modern civilization; but for the Theosophist, all its bounties can hardly repay for the evils it has brought on the world. These are so many, that it is not within the limits of this article to enumerate these offsprings of culture and of the progress of physical science, whose latest achievements begin with vivisection and end in improved murder by electricity.

Our answer, we have no doubt, is not calculated to make us more friends than enemies, but this can be hardly helped. Our magazine may be looked upon as 'pessimistic' but no one can charge it with publishing slanders or lies, or, in fact, anything but that which we honestly believe to be true. Be it as it may, however, we hope never to lack moral courage in the expression of our opinions or in defense of Theosophy and its society. Let then nine-tenths of every population arise in arms against the Theosophical Society wherever it appears—they will never be able to suppress the truths it utters. Let the masses of growing Materialism, the hosts of Spiritualism, all the Church-going congregations, bigots and iconoclasts, Grundy-worshippers, aping-followers and blind disciples, let them slander, abuse, lie, denounce, and publish every falsehood about us under the sun—they will not uproot Theosophy, nor even upset her Society, if only its members hold together. Let even such friends and *advisers* as he who is now answered, turn away in disgust from those whom he addresses in vain—it matters not, for our two paths in life run diametrically opposite. Let him keep to his terrestrial' wisdom; we will keep to that pure ray "that comes from above", from the light of the "Ancient".

What indeed, has WISDOM, *Theosophia*—the Wisdom "full of mercy and good fruits, without wrangling or partiality, and without hypocrisy" (James iii, 17)—to do with our cruel, selfish, crafty, and hypocritical world? What is there in common between divine Sophia and the improvements of modern civilization and science; between spirit and the letter that killeth? The more so as at this stage of evolution the wisest man on earth, according to the wise Carlyle, is "but a clever infant spelling letters from a hieroglyphical, prophetic book, the lexicon of which lies in *eternity*".

STUDIES IN OCCULTISM

A Series of Reprints from the Writings

of

H. P. BLAVATSKY

NO. V

THE ESOTERIC CHARACTER
OF
THE GOSPELS

THE ESOTERIC CHARACTER
OF THE GOSPELS

".... Tell us, when shall these things be? And what shall be the sign *of thy presence,* and *of the consummation of the age?* " [1] asked the Disciples of the MASTER, on the Mount of Olives.

THE reply given by the. "Man of Sorrows", the *Chrēstos,* on his trial, but also on his way to triumph, as *Christos,* or Christ, [2] is prophetic, and very suggestive. It is a warning indeed. The answer must be quoted in full. Jesus .... said unto them:—

"Take heed that *no man* lead you astray. For many shall come in my name saying, I am the Christ; and shall lead many astray. And ye shall hear of wars .... but the end is not yet. *For nation shall rise against nation, and kingdom against kingdom; and there shall be famines and earthquakes in divers places.* But all these things are the beginning of travail. . . . Many false prophets shall arise, and shall lead many astray. . . . . then shall the end come. . . . when ye see the abomination of desolation which was spoken through Daniel. . . Then if any man shall say unto you, *Lo, here is the Christ,* or there; believe him not. . . . If they shall say unto you, Behold, he is in the wilderness, go not forth; behold, he is in the inner chambers, believe them not. For as the lightning cometh forth from the East, and is seen even in the West, so shall be the *presence* of the Son of Man," etc.

Two things become evident *to all* in the above passages, now that their false rendering is corrected in the revision text: *(a)* "the coming of Christ", means *the presence of* CHRISTOS in a regenerated world, and not at all the actual coming in body of 'Christ' Jesus; *(b)* this Christ is to be sought neither in the wilderness nor "in the inner chambers", nor in the sanctuary of any temple or church built by man; for Christ—the true esoteric SAVIOR—is *no man,* but the DIVINE PRINCIPLE in every human being. He who strives to resurrect the Spirit *crucified in him by his own terrestrial passions,* and buried deep in the 'sepulchre' of his sinful flesh; he who has the strength to roll back *the stone of matter* from the door of his own *inner* sanctuary, he *has the risen Christ in him.* [3] The "Son of Man" is no child of the bond-woman—*flesh,* but verily of the free-woman— *Spirit,* [4] the child of man's own deeds, and the fruit of his own spiritual labor.

On the other hand, at no time since the Christian era, have the precursor signs described in *Matthew* applied so graphically and forcibly to any epoch as they do to our own times. When has nation arisen against nation more than at this time? When have 'famines'—another name for destitute pauperism, and the famished multitudes of the proletariat—been more cruel, earthquakes more frequent, or covered such an area simultaneously, as for the last few years? Millenarians and

---

[1] *St. Matthew xxiv,* 3, *et seq.* The sentences italicised are those which stand corrected in the New Testament after the recent revision in 1881 of the version of 1611; which version is full of errors, voluntary and involuntary. The word "presence" for "coming" and "the consummation of the age" now standing for "the end of the world", have altered, of late, the whole meaning, even for the most sincere Christians, if we exempt the Adventists.

[2] He who will not ponder over and master the great difference between the meaning of the two Greek word—χρηστος and χριστος must remain blind forever to the true esoteric meaning of the Gospels; that is to say, to the living Spirit entombed in the sterile dead-letter of the texts, the very Dead Sea fruit of *lip*-Christianity.

[3] For ye are the temple ('sanctuary' in the *revised* N. T.) of the living God. II Cor. vi, 16.

[4] Spirit, or the Holy Ghost, was feminine with the Jews, as with most ancient peoples, and it was so with the early Christians. *Sophia* of the Gnostics, and the third Sephiroth *Binah* (the *female* Jehovah of the Kabalists), are feminine principles—"Divine Spirit", or *Ruach. "Achath Ruach Elohim Chiim."* "One is *She,* the Spirit of the Elohim of Life", is said in *Sepher Yezirah.*

Adventists of robust faith may go on saying that "the coming of (the carnalized) Christ" is near at hand, and prepare themselves for "the end of the world". Theosophists—at any rate, some of them—who understand the hidden meaning of the universally expected Avatars, Messiahs, Sosioshes, and Christs—know that it is no "end of the world", but "the consummation of the age", *i.e.,* the close of a cycle, which is now fast approaching.[1] If our readers have forgotten the concluding passages of the article, "The Signs of the Times",[2] in LUCIFER for October last, let them read them over, and they will see the meaning of this particular cycle.

Many and many a time the warning about the "false Christs" and prophets who shall lead people astray has been interpreted by charitable Christians, the worshippers of the dead-letter of their scripture, as applying to mystics generally, and Theosophists most especially. The recent work by Mr. Pember, *Earth's Earliest Ages, is* a proof of it. Nevertheless, it seems very evident that the words in Matthew's Gospel and others can hardly apply to Theosophists. For these were never found *saying* that Christ is 'Here' or 'There', in wilderness or city, and least of all in the "inner chamber" behind the altar of any modern church. Whether Heathen or Christian by birth, they refuse to materialize and thus degrade that which is the purest and grandest ideal—the symbol of symbols—namely, the immortal Divine Spirit in man, whether it be called Horus, Krishna, Buddha, or Christ. None of them has ever yet said: "I am the Christ"; for those born in the West feel themselves, so far, only *Chréstlam,*[3] however much they may strive to become *Christiana* in Spirit. It is to those, who in their great conceit and pride refuse to win the right to such appellation by first leading the life of *Chrestos;*[4] to those who haughtily proclaim themselves *Christians* (the glorified, the anointed) by sole virtue of baptism when but a few days old—that the above-quoted words of Jesus apply most forcibly. Can the prophetic insight of him who uttered this remarkable warning be doubted by anyone who sees the numerous "false prophets" and pseudo-apostles *(of Christ)* now roaming over the world? These have split the one divine Truth into fragments, and broken, in the camp of the Protestants alone, the rock of the Eternal Verity into three hundred and fifty odd pieces, which now represent the bulk of their dissenting sects. Accepting the number in round figures as 350, and admitting, for argument's sake, that at least one of these may have the approximate truth, still *349 must be necessarily false.*[5] Each of

---

[1] There are several remarkable cycles that come to a close at the end of this century. First the 5,000 years of the *Katiyug* cycle; again, the Messianic cycle of the Samaritan (also Kabalistic) Jews of the man connected with *Pisces* (Ichthys or 'Fishman' *Dag*). *It is* a cycle, historic and not very long, but very occult, lasting about 2,155 solar years, but having a true significance only when computed by lunar months. It occurred 2410 and 255 B.C., or when the equinox entered into the sign of the *Rant,* and again into that of *Pisces.* When it enters, in a few years, the sign of *Aquarius,* psychologists will have some extra work to do, and the psychic idiosyncrasies of humanity will enter on a great change.

[2] See No. I of this Series.

[3] The earliest Christian author, Justin Martyr, calls, in in his first Apology, his co-religionists *Chrestians,* χρηστιανοι—not Christians.

[4] "Clemens Alexandrinus, in the second century, founds a serious argument on his paranomasia (lib. iii, cap. xvii, p. 53 *et circa),* that all who believed in *Chrest (i.e.,* "a good man") both are, and are called Chrestians, that is, good men", (Strommata, lib. ii, "Higgins' *Anacalypsis").* And Lactantius (lib. iv, cap. vii) says that it is only through *ignorance* that people call themselves Christians instead of Chrestians: *"qui proper ignorantium errorem cum immutato. litera Chrestum solent dicere".*

[5] In England alone there are 239 various sects. (See Whitaker's Almanac.) In 1883 there were 188

these claims to have Christ exclusively in its "inner chamber", and denies him to all others, while, in truth, the great majority of their respective followers daily put Christ to death on the cruciform tree of matter—the "tree of infamy" of the old Romans—indeed!

The worship of the dead-letter in the Bible is but one more form of *idolatry,* nothing better. A fundamental dogma of faith cannot exist under a double-faced Janus form. 'Justification' *by Christ* cannot be achieved at one's choice and fancy, *either* by 'faith' or by 'works', and James, therefore (ii, 25), contradicting Paul (Heb. xi, 31), and *vice versa,* [1] one of them must be wrong. Hence the Bible is *not* "Word of God", but contains at best the words of fallible men and *imperfect* teachers. Yet read *esoterically,* it does contain, if not the *whole* truth, still, *"nothing but the truth",* under what-whatever allegorical garb. Only: *Quot homines tot sententiœ*

The " Christ principle", the awakened and glorified Spirit of Truth, being universal and eternal, the true *Christos* cannot be monopolized by any one person, even though that person has chosen to arrogate to himself the title of the "Vicar of Christ", or of the 'Head' of that or another State-religion. The spirits of 'Chrest' and 'Christ' cannot be confined to any creed or sect, only because that sect chooses to exalt itself above the heads of all other religions or sects. The name has been used in a manner so intolerant and dogmatic, especially in our day, that Christianity is now the religion of arrogance *par excellence,* a stepping-stone for ambition, a sinecure for wealth, sham, and power; a convenient screen for hypocrisy. The noble epithet of old, the one that made Justin Martyr say that *"from the mere name, which is imputed to us as a crime, we are the most excellent,"*[2] is now degraded. The missionary prides himself with the so-called *conversion* of a heathen, who makes of Christianity ever a *profession,* but rarely a religion, a source of income from the missionary fund, and a pretext, since the blood of Jesus has washed them all, by anticipation, for every petty crime, from drunkenness and lying up to theft. That same missionary, however, would not hesitate to publicly condemn the greatest saint to eternal perdition and hell fires if that holy man had only neglected to pass through the fruitless and meaningless form of baptism by water with accompaniment of *lip* prayers and vain ritualism.

We say "lip prayer" and "vain ritualism" knowingly. Few Christians among the laymen are aware even of the true meaning of the word *Christ;* and those of the clergy who happen to know it (for they are brought up in the idea that to study such subjects is *sinful*) keep the information secret from their parishioners. They demand blind, implicit faith, and *forbid inquiry as the one unpardonable sin,* though nothing of that which leads to the knowledge of the truth can be aught else than holy. For what is "Divine Wisdom", or *Gnosis,* but the essential reality behind the evanescent appearances of objects in nature—the very soul of the

---

denominations only, and now they steadily increase with every year, an additional fifty-three sects having sprung up in only four years!

[1] It is but fair to St. Paul to remark that this contradiction is surely due to later tampering with his Epistles. Paul was a Gnostic himself, *i.e., a* "Son of Wisdom", and an initiate into the true *? mysteries of Christos,* though he may *have* thundered (or was made to appear to do so) against some Gnostic sects, of which, in his day, there were many. But his Christos was not Jesus of Nazareth, nor any living man, as shown so ably in Mr. Gerald Massey's lecture, "Paul, the Gnostic Opponent of Peter". He was an Initiate, a true "Master-Builder" or adept, as described in *"Isis* Unveiled", Vol. II, pp. 90-91.

[2] ὅσοντε ἐκ τôυ κατηγαρουμένου ἡμῶν ὀνόματος χρησότατοι ὑπάρχομεν *(First Apology).*

manifested LOGOS? Why should men who strive to accomplish union with the one eternal and absolute Deity shudder at the idea of prying into its mysteries— however awful? Why, above all, should they use names and words the very meaning of which is a sealed mystery to them—a mere sound? Is it because an unscrupulous, power-seeking Establishment called a Church has cried 'wolf' at every such attempt, and, denouncing it as 'blasphemous', has ever tried to kill the spirit of inquiry? But Theosophy, the "divine Wisdom", has never heeded that cry, and has the courage of its opinions. The world of sceptics and fanatics may call it: one—an empty *'ism'*: the other—'Satanism'. They can never crush it. Theosophists have been called Atheists, haters of Christianity, the enemies of God and the gods. They are none of these. Therefore, they have agreed this day to publish a clear statement of their ideas, and a profession of their faith—with regard to monotheism and Christianity, at any rate—and to place it before the impartial reader to judge them and their detractors on the merits of their respective faiths. No truth-loving mind would object to such honest and sincere dealing, nor will it be dazzled by any amount of new light thrown upon the subject, howsoever much startled otherwise. On the contrary, such minds will thank LUCIFER, perhaps, while those of whom it was said *"qui vult decipi decipiatur"*—*let* them be deceived by all means!

The editors of this magazine propose to give a series of essays upon the hidden meaning or esotericism of the "New Testament". No more than any other scripture of the great world-religions can the Bible be excluded from that class of allegorical and symbolical writings which have been, from the pre-historic ages the receptacle of the secret teachings of the Mysteries of Initiation, under a more or less veiled form. The primitive writers of the *Logia* (now the Gospels) knew certainly *the* truth, and the *whole* truth; but their successors had, as certainly, only dogma and form, which lead to hierarchical power at heart, rather than the spirit of the so-called Christ's teachings. Hence the gradual perversion. As Higgins truly said, in the Christologia of St. Paul and Justin Martyr, we have the esoteric religion of the Vatican, a refined Gnosticism for the cardinals, a more gross one for the people. It is the latter, only still more materialized and disfigured, which has reached us in our age.

The idea of writing this series was suggested to us by a certain letter published in our October issue, under the heading of "Are the Teachings ascribed to Jesus contradictory?" Nevertheless, this is no attempt to contradict or weaken, in any one instance, that which was said by Mr. Gerald Massey in his criticism. The contradictions pointed out by the learned lecturer and author are too patent to be explained away by any 'preacher' or Bible champion; for what he has said—only in more terse and vigorous language—is what was said of the descendant of Joseph Pandira (or Panthera) in *Isis Unveiled* (vol. ii, p. 201), from the Talmudic *Sepher Toldos ,Jeshu.* His belief with regard to the spurious character of Bible and New Testament, *as now edited,* is therefore, also the belief of the present writer. In view of the recent revision of the Bible, and its many thousands of mistakes, mistranslations, and interpolations (some confessed to, and others withheld), it would ill become an opponent to take any one to task for refusing to believe in the authorized texts.

But the editors would object to one short sentence in the criticism under notice. Mr. Gerald Massey writes:—

"What is the use of taking your 'Bible oath' that the thing is true, if the book you are sworn upon is a magazine of falsehoods already exploded, or just going off?"

Surely it is not a symbologist of Mr. G. Massey's powers and learning who would call the *Book of the Dead,* or the *Vedas,* or any other ancient Scripture, "a magazine of falsehoods".[1] Why not regard in the same light as all the others, the Old, and, in a *still greater measure,* the *New* Testament?

All of these are "magazines of falsehoods", if accepted in the exoteric dead-letter interpretations of their ancient, and especially their modern theological glossarists. Each of these records has served in its turn as a means for securing power and of supporting the ambitious policy of an unscrupulous priesthood. All have promoted superstition, all made of their gods bloodthirsty and ever-damning Molochs and fiends, as all have made nations to serve the latter more than the God of Truth. But while cunningly-devised dogmas and intentional misinterpretations by scholiasts are beyond any doubt, "falsehoods already exploded", the texts themselves are mines of universal truths. But for the world of the profane and sinners, at any rate—they were and still are like the mysterious characters traced by "the fingers of a man's hand" on the wall of the Palace of Belshazzar: *they need a Daniel to read and understand them.*

Nevertheless, TRUTH has not allowed herself to remain without witnesses. There are, besides great Initiates into scriptural symbology, a number of quiet students of the mysteries of archaic esotericism, of scholars proficient in Hebrew and other dead tongues, who have devoted their lives to unriddle the speeches of the Sphinx of the world-religions. And these students, though none of them has yet mastered all the "seven keys" that open the great problem, have discovered enough to be able to say: There *was* a universal mystery-language, in which all the World-Scriptures were written, from *Vedas* to *Revelation,* from the *Book of the Dead* to the *Acts.* One of the keys, at any rate—the numerical and geometrical key[2]—to the Mystery Speech is now rescued; an ancient language, truly, which up to this time remained hidden, but the evidences of which abundantly exist, as may be proven by undeniable mathematical demonstrations. If, indeed, the Bible is forced on the acceptance of the world in its dead-letter meaning, in the face of the modern discoveries by Orientalists and the efforts of independent students and kabalists, it is easy to prophesy that even the present new generations of Europe and America

---

[1] The extraordinary amount of information collated by that able Egyptologist shows that he has thoroughly mastered the secret of the production of the *New Testament.* Mr. Massey knows the difference between the spiritual, divine, and purely metaphysical Christos, and the made-up "lay figure" of the carnalized Jesus. He knows also that the Christian canon, especially the *Gospels, Acts,* and *Epistles,* are made up of fragments of gnostic wisdom, the ground-work of which is *pre-Christian* and built on the MYSTERIES of Initiation. It is the mode of theological presentation, and the interpolated passages—such as in *Mark* xvi, from verse 9 to the end—which make of the *Gospels* a "magazine of *(wicked)* falsehoods", and throw a slur on CHRISTOS. But the occultist who discerns between the two currents (the true gnostic and the *pseudo* Christian) knows that the passages free from theological tampering belong to archaic wisdom, and so does Mr. Gerald Massey, though his views differ from ours.

[2] "The key to the recovery of the language, so far as the writer's efforts have been concerned, was found in the use, strange to say, of the discovered integral ratio in numbers of diameter to circumference of a circle," by a geometrician. "This ratio is 6,561 for diameter and 20,612 for circumference." (Cabalistic MSS.) In one of the future numbers of LUCIFER more details will be given, with the permission of the discoverer.—ED.

will repudiate it, as all the materialists and logicians have done. For, the more one studies ancient religious texts, the more one finds that the ground-work of the New Testament is the same as the groundwork of the *Vedas*, of the Egyptian theogony, and the Mazdean allegories. The atonements by blood—blood-covenants and blood-transferences from gods to men, and by men as sacrifices to the gods—are the first key-note struck in every cosmogony and theogony; soul, life, and blood were synonymous words in every language, preeminently with the Jews; and that blood-giving was life-giving. "Many a legend among (geographically) alien nations ascribes soul and consciousness in newly-created mankind to the blood of the god creators. Berosus records a Chaldean legend ascribing the creation of a new race of mankind to the admixture of dust with the blood that flowed from the severed head of the god Belus. "On this account it is that men are rational and partake of divine knowledge", explains Berosus.[1] And Lenormant has shown *(Beginnings of History,* p.52, note) that "the Orphics . . . . said that the *immaterial part of man, his soul* (his life) sprang from the blood of Dionysius Zagreus, whom . . . Titans tore to pieces". Blood "revivifies the dead"—*i.e.,* interpreted metaphysically, it gives *conscious* life and a soul to the man of matter or clay—such as the modern materialist is now. The mystic meaning of the injunction, "verily I *say* unto you, except *ye eat the flesh* of the Son of man and *drink his blood,* ye have not life in yourselves," etc., can never be understood or appreciated at its true *occult* value, except by those who hold some of the *seven keys,* and yet care little for St. Peter.[2] These words, whether said by Jesus of Nazareth, or Jeshua Ben-Panthera, are the words of an INITIATE. They have to be interpreted with the help of *three* keys—one opening the *psychic* door, the second that of physiology, and the third, that which unlocks the mystery of terrestrial being, by unveiling the inseparable blending of theogony with anthropology. It is for revealing a few of these truths, with the *sole view of saving intellectual mankind from the insanities of materialism and pessimism,* that mystics have often been denounced as the servants of Antichrist, even by those Christians who are most worthy, sincerely pious, and respectable men.

The first key that one has to use to unravel the dark secrets involved in the mystic name of Christ, is the key which unlocked the door to the ancient mysteries of the primitive Aryans, Sabeans, and Egyptians. The Gnosis supplanted by the Christian scheme was universal. It was the echo of the primordial wisdom-religion

---

[1] Cory's *Ans. Frail.,* p. 59, f. So do Sanchoniaton and Hesiod, who both ascribe the *vivifying* of mankind to the spilt blood of the gods. But blood and *soul* are one *(nephesh),* and the blood of the gods means here the informing soul.

[2] The existence of these *seven* keys is virtually admitted, owing to deep research in the Egyptological lore, by Mr. G. Massey again. While opposing the teachings of *Esoteric Buddhism—unfortunately* misunderstood by him in almost every respect—in his lecture on "The Seven Souls of Man", he writes, (p. 21):—

"This system of thought, this mode of representation, this septenary of powers, in various aspects, had been established in Egypt, at least, seven thousand years ago, as we learn from certain allusions to Atum (the god 'in whom the fatherhood was individualized as the *begetter of an eternal soul,'* the *seventh* principle of the Theosophists, found in the inscriptions lately discovered at Sakkarah. I say in various aspects, *because the gnosis of the Mysteries was,* at least, *sevenfold in its nature—it* was Elemental, Biological, Elementary (human), Stellar, Lunar, Solar, and Spiritual—and *nothing short of a grasp of the whole system can possibly enable us to discriminate the various parts, distinguish one from the other, and determinate the which and the what, as we try to follow the symbolical Seven through their several phases of character.*"

which had once been the heirloom of the whole of mankind; and, therefore, one may truly say that, in its purely metaphysical aspect, the Spirit of Christ (the divine *logos)* was present in humanity from the beginning of it. The author of the Clementine Homilies is right; the mystery of Christos—now supposed to have been taught by Jesus of Nazareth—"was identical" with that which *from the first* had been communicated *"to those who were worthy",* as quoted in another lecture.[1] We may learn from the Gospel *according* to Luke, that the "worthy" were those who had been initiated into the mysteries of the Gnosis, and who were "accounted worthy" to attain that "resurrection from the dead" *in this life,* . . . . "those who knew that they could die no more, being equal to the angels as sons of God and sons of the Resurrection". In other words, they were the great adepts *of whatever religion ;* and the words apply to all those who, without being Initiates, strive and succeed, through personal efforts to *live the life* and to attain the naturally ensuing spiritual illumination in blending their personality—the "Son" with the "Father", their individual divine Spirit, *the God within* them. This "resurrection" can never be monopolized by the Christians, but is the spiritual birth-right of every human being endowed with soul and spirit, whatever his religion may be. Such individual is a *Christ-man.* On the other hand, those who choose to ignore the Christ (principle) within themselves, must die *unregenerate heathens—baptism,* sacraments, lip-prayers, and belief in dogmas notwithstanding.

In order to follow this explanation, the reader must bear in mind the real archaic meaning of the paranomisia involved in the two terms *Chréstos* and *Christos.* The former means certainly more than merely a "good", an "excellent man", while the latter was never applied to any one living man, but to every Initiate at the moment of *his second birth and resurrection.*[2] He who finds Christos within himself and recognises the latter as his only "way", becomes a follower and an *Apostle of Christ,* though he may have never been baptised, nor even have met a "Christian", still less call himself one.

---

[1] "Gnostic and Historic Christianity."

[2] "Verily, verily, I say unto thee, except a man *be born again* he cannot see the kingdom of God." (John iii, 4.) Here the birth *from above,* the spiritual birth, is meant, achieved at the supreme and last initiation.

II

THE word Chréstos existed ages before Christianity was heard of. It is found used, from the fifth century B.C., by Herodotus, by Æschylus, and other classical Greek writers, the meaning of it being applied to both things and persons.

Thus in Æschylus (Cho. 901) we read of Μαντεύματα πυθόχρηστα *(pytho-chrésta)* the "oracles delivered by a Pythian God" *(Greek-English Lexicon)* through a pythoness; and *Pythochréstos* is the nominative singular of an adjective derived from *chrao χράω* (Eurip. *Ion,* 1,218). The later meanings, coined freely from this primitive application are numerous and varied. Pagan classics expressed more than one idea by the verb χράομαι, "consulting an oracle"; for it also means " fated", *doomed by* an oracle, in the sense of a *sacrificial victim to its decree,* or— "to the WORD"; as *chrésterion,* is not only "the seat of an oracle" but also "an offering to, or for, the oracle".[1] *Chrestés, χρήστης,* is one who expounds or explains oracles, "a *prophet, a soothsayer;"*[2] and *chresterios, χρμστήριος,* is one who belongs to, or is in the service of an oracle, a god, or a "Master";[3] this Canon Far-rar's efforts notwithstanding.[4]

All this is evidence that the terms Christ and Christians, spelt originally *Christ* and *Chréstians, χρηστιανοι,*[5] were directly borrowed from the Temple terminology of the Pagans, and meant the same thing. The God of the Jews was now substituted for the Oracle and the other gods; the generic designation "Chréstos" became a noun applied to one special personage; and new terms such as *Chréstianoï* and *Chréstodoulos* "a follower or servant of Chrestos"—were coined out of the old material. This is shown by Philo Judæus, a monotheist, assuredly, using already the same term for monotheistic purposes. For he speaks of θεόχρηστος

---

[1] The word χρεών is explained by Herodotus (7, 11, 7,) as that which an oracle declares, and τὸ χρεών is given by Plutarch (Nic. 14.) as "fate", "necessity". *Vide* Herod, 7, 215; 5, 108; and Sophocles, Phil., 437.

[2] See Liddell and Scott's Greek-English Lexicon.

[3] Hence of a *Guru,* "a teacher" and *chela,* a "disciple", in their mutual relations.

[4] In his recent work—*The Early Days of Christianity,* Canon Farrar remarks:—"Some have supposed a pleasant play of words founded on it, as . . . . between *Chréstos* ('sweet' Ps., xxx, iv, 8) and Christos (Christ)", (I, p. 158, *foot-note).* But there is nothing to suppose, since it began by a "play of words", indeed. The name *Christus* was *not* "distorted into Chrestus", as the learned author would make his readers believe (p. 19), but it was the adjective and noun *Chréstos* which became distorted into *Christus,* and applied to Jesus. In a foot-note on the word "Chrestian", occurring in the *First Epistle* of Peter (chap. iv, 16), in which the *revised* later MSS. the word was changed into *Christian,* Canon Farrar remarks again, "Perhaps we should read the ignorant heathen distortion, *Chréstian".* Most decidedly we should; for the eloquent writer should remember his Master's command to renderunto Cæsar that which is Cæsar's. His dislike notwithstanding, Mr. Farrar is obliged to admit that the name *Christian* was first INVENTED by the sneering, mocking Antiochians, as early as A.D. 44, but had not come into general use before the persecution by Nero. "Tacitus", he says, "uses the word 'Christians' with something of apology. It is well known that in the N.T. it only occurs three times, and always involves a hostile sense *(Acts, xi,* 26,xxvi, 28, as it does in iv, 16)". It was not Claudius alone who looked with alarm and suspicion on the Christians, so nicknamed in derision for their carnalizing a subjective principle or attribute, but all the pagan nations. For Tacitus, speaking of those whom the masses called "Christians", describes them as a set of men *detested for their enormities* and crimes. No wonder, for history repeats itself. There are, no doubt, thousands of noble, sincere, and virtuous *Christian-born* men and women now. But we have only to look at the viciousness of Christian "heathen" converts; at the *morality* of those proselytes in India, whom the missionaries themselves decline to take into their service, to draw a parallel between the converts of 1,800 years ago, and the modern heathens "touched *by grace".*

[5] Justin Martyr, Tertullian, Lactantius, Clemens Alexandrinus, and others spelt it in this way.

(théochréstos) "God-declared", or one who is declared by God, and of λόγια θεόχρηστα *(logic théochrésta)* "sayings delivered by God"—which proves that he wrote at a time (between the first century B.C., and the first A.D.) when neither Christians nor Chrestians were yet known under these names, but still called themselves the Nazarenes. The notable difference between the two words χράω— "consulting or obtaining response from a god or oracle" (χρεω, being the Ionic earlier form of it)—and χριω, *(chrio)* "to rub, to anoint" (from which the name Christos), have not prevented the ecclesiastical adoption and coinage from Philo's expression θεόχρηστος of that other term θεόχριστος, "anointed by God". Thus the quiet substitution of the letter ι for η for dogmatic purposes, was achieved in the easiest way, as we now see.

The secular meaning of *Chréstos* runs throughout the classical Greek literature *pari passu* with that given to it in the mysteries. Demosthenes' saying ὦ χρηστέ (330, 27), means by it simply "you nice fellow"; Plato (in Phaed. 264 B) has χρηστός εἶ ὅτι ἡγεῖ—"you are an excellent fellow to think . . ." But in the esoteric phraseology of the temples "chrestos",[1] a word which, like the participle *chréstheis,* is formed under the same rule, and conveys the same sense—from the verb χράομαι ("to consult a god")—answers to what we would call an adept, also a high *chela,* a disciple. It is in this sense that it is used by Euripides *(Ion,* 1320) and by Æschylus (1 c). This qualification was applied to those whom the god, oracle, or any superior had proclaimed this, that, or anything else. An instance may be given in this case.

The words χρεσεν οικιστῆρα used by Pindar (pp. 4-10) mean "the oracle *proclaimed* him the colonizer". In this case the genius of the Greek language permits that the man so proclaimed should be called χρεστός *(Chréstos).* Hence this term was applied to every Disciple recognised by a Master, as also to every good man. Now the Greek language affords strange etymologies. Christian theology has chosen and decreed that the name Christos should be taken as derived from χρίΩ, χρίσω (Chriso), "anointed with scented unguents or oil". But this word has several significances. It is used by Homer, certainly, as applied to the rubbing with oil of the body after bathing *(Il.,* 23, 186; also in *Od.,* 4, 252) as other ancient writers do. Yet the word χρίστης *(Christes)* means rather a *whitewasher,* while the word χρήστης *(Chrestes)* means priest and prophet, a term far more applicable to Jesus than that of the "Anointed", since, as Nork shows on the authority of the Gospels, he never was anointed, either as king or priest. In short, there is a deep mystery underlying all this scheme, which, as I maintain, only a thorough knowledge of the *Pagan* mysteries is capable of unveiling.[2] It is not what the early

---

[1] *Vide* Liddell and Scott's Greek and English Lexicon. *Chréstos* is really one who is continually warned, advised guided, whether by oracle or prophet. Mr. G. Massey is not correct in saying that ". . . . The Gnostic form of the name Chrest, or Chrestos, denotes the *Good God,* not a human original," for it denoted the latter, i. e., a good, holy man; but he is quite right when he adds that" *Chrestianas* signifies . . . . 'Sweetness and Light'". "The *Chrestoi,* as the *Good People,* were pre-extant. Numerous Greek inscriptions show that the departed, the hero, the saintly one—that is, the 'Good'—was styled *Chrestos,* or the Christ; and from this meaning of the 'Good' does Justin, the primal apologist, derive the Christian name. This identifies it with the Gnostic source, and with the 'Good God' who revealed himself according to Marcionthat is, the Un-Nefer or Good-opener of the Egyptian theology."— *(Agnostic Annual.)*

[2] Again I must bring forward what Mr. G. Massey says (whom I quote repeatedly because he has studied this subject so thoroughly and so conscientiously).

"My contention, or rather explanation", he says, "is that the author of the Christian name is the

---

Fathers, who had an object to achieve, may affirm or deny, that is the important point, but rather what is now the evidence for the real significance given to the two terms *Chréstos* and *Christos by* the ancients in the pre-Christian ages. For the latter had no object to achieve, therefore nothing to conceal or disfigure, and their evidence is naturally the more reliable of the two. This evidence can be obtained by first studying the meaning given to these words by the classics, and then their correct significance searched for in mystic symbology.

Now *Chrestos,* as already said, is a term applied in various senses. It qualifies both Deity and Man. It is used in the former sense in the Gospels, and in Luke (vi., 35), where it means "kind" and "merciful". Χρηστόσ ἐστιν ἐπὶ τοὺς, in I Peter (ii, 3), where it is said, "Kind is the Lord", χρεστὸς ὁ κύριος. On the other hand, it is explained by Clemens Alexandrinus as simply meaning a good man; *i.e.* "All who believe in *Chrést* (a good man) both *are,* and *are called Chréstians,* that is, good men" (Strom. lib. ii). The reticence of Clemens, whose Christianity, as King truly remarks in his *Gnostics,* was no more than a graft upon the congenial stock of his original Platonism, is quite natural. He was an Initiate, a new Platonist, before he became a Christian, which fact, however much he may have fallen off from his earlier views, could not exonerate him from his pledge of secrecy. And as a Theosophist and a *Gnostic,* one who *knew,* Clemens must have known that *Christos* was "the WAY", while *Chrestos* was the lonely traveller journeying on to reach the ultimate goal through that "Path", which goal was *Christos,* the glorified Spirit of "TRUTH", the reunion with which makes the soul (the Son) ONE with the (Father) Spirit. That Paul knew it is certain, for his own expressions prove it. For what do the words πάλιν ὠδίνω, ἄχρις οὗ μορφωθῆ χριστὸς ἐνὑμῖν, or, as given in the authorized translations, " I am again in travail until *Christ be formed in you"* mean, but what we give in its esoteric rendering, *i.e.,* "until you find *the* Christos within yourselves as your only 'way'". (*Vide* Galatians iv, 19 and 20.)

Thus Jesus, whether of Nazareth or Lüd,[1] was a Chréstos, as undeniably as that he never was entitled to the appellation of *Christos,* during his life-time and before his last trial. It may have been as Higgins thinks, who surmises that the first name of Jesus was, perhaps, χρεισος, the second, χρησος, and the third χρισος. "The word χρεισος was in use before the H (cap. *eta)* was in the language." But Taylor (in his answer to Pye Smith, p. 113) is quoted saying "The complimentary epithet Christ . . . . signified nothing more than a good man".

Here again a number of ancient writers may be brought forward to testify that *Christos* (or *Chreistos,* rather) was, along with χρησος = Hrésos, an adjective

---

Mummy-Christ of Egypt, called the *Karest,* which was a type of the immortal spirit in man, the Christ within (as Paul has it), the divine offspring incarnated, the Logos, the Word of Truth, the *Makheru* of Egypt. It did not originate as a mere type! The preserved mummy was the *dead body of anyone* that was *Karest,* or mummified, to be kept by the living; and, through constant repetition, this became *a* type of the resurrection from (not of!) the dead." See the explanation of this further on.

[1] Of Lydda. Reference is made here to the Rabbinical tradition in the Babylonian Gemara, called *Sepher Toledoth Jeshu,* about Jesus being the son of one named Pandira, and having lived a century earlier than the era called Christian, namely, during the reign of the Jewish king Alexander Jannæus and his wife Salome, who reigned from the year 106 to 79 B. C. Accused by the Jews of having learned the magic art in Egypt, and of having stolen from the Holy of Holies the Incommunicable Name, Jehoshna (Jesus), was put to death by the Sanhedrin at Lüd. He was stoned and then crucified on a tree, on the eve of Passover. The narrative is ascribed to the Talmudistic authors of *Sota* and *Sanhedrin,* p.19, Rook of Zechiel. See *Isis Untvelled,*II, 201; Arnobius; Eliphas Levi's *Science des Esprits,* and *The Historical Jesus and Mythical Christ,* a lecture by G. Massey.

applied to Gentiles before the Christian era. In *Philopatris* it is said εἰ τύχοι χρηστός καὶ ἐν ἔθνεαιν, *i.e.*, "if chrestos chance to be even among the Gentiles", *etc.*

Tertullian denounces in the third chapter of his *Apologia* the word *"Christianus"* as derived by "crafty interpretation";[1] Dr. Jones, on the other hand, letting out the information, corroborated by good sources, that *"Hrésos (χρησός)* was the name given to Christ by the Gnostics, and even by unbelievers," assures us that the real name ought to be χρισός or *Chrisos*—*thus* repeating and supporting the original "pious fraud" of the early Fathers, a fraud which led to the carnalizing of the whole Christian system.[2] But I propose to show as much of the real meaning of all these terms as lies within my humble powers and knowledge. Christos, or the "Christ-condition", was ever the synonym of the "Mahatmic-condition", *i.e.*, the union of the man with the divine principle in him. As Paul says (Ephes. iii, 17) *"κατοικῆσαι τὸν χριστόν διὰ τῆς πίστεως ἐν ταῖς καρδίαις ὑμῶν".* "That you may find Christos in your *inner* man through *knowledge"* not faith, as translated; for *Pistis is* "knowledge", as will be shown further on.

There is still another and far more weighty proof that the name *Christos* is pre-Christian. The evidence for it is found in the prophecy of the Erythrean Sybil. We read it in ΊΗΣΟΥΣ ΧΡΕΙΣΤΟΣ ΘΕΟΝ ΎΙΟΣ ΣΩΤΗΡ ΣΤΑΥΡΟΣ. Read esoterically, this string of meaningless detached nouns, which has no sense to the profane, contains a real prophecy—only not referring to Jesus—and a verse from the mystic catechism of the Initiate. The prophecy relates to the coming down upon the Earth of the Spirit of Truth (Christos), after which advent—that has once more naught to do with Jesus—will begin the Golden Age; the verse refers to the necessity before reaching that blessed condition of inner (or subjective) theophany and theopneusty, to pass through the crucifixion of flesh or matter. Read esoterically, the words *Iesous Chreistos theon yios soter stauros,* meaning literally "Iesus, Christos, God, Son, Savior, Cross", are most excellent handles to hang a Christian prophecy on, but they are *pagan,* not Christian.

If called upon to explain the name IESOUS CHREISTOS, the answer is: study mythology, the so-called "fictions" of the ancients, and they will give you the key. Ponder over Apollo, the solar god, and the "Healer", and the allegory about his son Janus (or Ion), his priest at Delphos, through whom alone could prayers reach the immortal gods, and his other son Asclepios, called the *Soter,* or Savior. Here is a leaflet from esoteric history written in symbological phraseology by the old Grecian poets.

The city of Chrisa[3] (now spelt Crisa), was built in memory of Kreusa (or Creu-

---

[1] Christians quantum interpretatione do unctione deducitas. Sed ut cum perferam Chrestianus pronunciatus a vobis (nam nec nominis certa est notitia penes vos) de suavitate vel benignitate compositum est." Canon Farrar makes a great effort to show such *lapsus calami* by various Fathers as the results of disgust and fear. "There can be little doubt", he says (in *The Early Days of christianity)* "that the ... name Christian .... was a nick-name due to the wit of the Antiochians It is clear that the sacred writers avoided the name (Christians) because it was employed by their enemies (Tao. Ann. xv, 44). It only became familiar when the virtues of Christians had shed lustre upon it. . . ." This is a very lame excuse, and a poor explanation to give for so eminent a thinker as Canon Farrar. As to the "virtues of Christians" ever shedding *lustre* upon the name, let us hope that the writer had in his mind's eye neither Bishop Cyril, of Alexandria, nor Eusebius, nor the Emperor Constantine, of murderous fame, nor yet the Popes Borgia and the Holy Inquisition.
[2] Quoted by G. Higgins. (See Vol. I, pp. 569-573.)
[3] In the days of Homer, we find this city, once celebrated for its mysteries, the chief seat of Initiation,

sa), daughter of King Erechtheus and mother of Janus or (Ion) by Apollo, in memory of the danger which Janus escaped.[1] We learn that Janus, abandoned by his mother in a grotto "to hide the shame of the virgin who bore a son", was found by Hermes, who brought the infant to Delphi, nurtured him by his father's sanctuary and oracle, where, under the name of Chresis (χρησις) Janus became first a *Chrestis* (a priest, soothsayer, or Initiate), and then very nearly a *Chrest-erion*, "a sacrificial victim",[2] ready to be poisoned by his own mother, who knew him not, and who, in her jealousy, mistook him, on the hazy intimation of the oracle, for a son of her husband. He pursued her to the very altar with the intention of killing her—when she was saved through the pythoness, who divulged to both the secret of their relationship. In memory of this narrow escape, Creusa, the mother, built the city of Chrisa, or Krisa. Such is the allegory, and it symbolizes simply the trials of Initiation.[3]

Finding then that Janus, the Solar God, and son of Apollo, the Sun, means the "Initiator" and the "Opener of the Gate of Light", or secret wisdom of the mysteries; that he is born from Krisa (esoterically *Chris*), and that he was a *Chrestos* through whom spoke the God; that he was finally Ion, the father of the Ionians, and some say, an *aspect* of Asclepios, another son of Apollo, it is easy to get hold of the thread of Ariadne in this labyrinth of allegories. It is not the place here to prove side issues in mythology, however. It suffices to show the connection between the mythical characters of hoary antiquity and the later fables that marked the beginning of our era of civilization. Asclepios (Esculapius) was the divine physician, the "Healer", the "Savior", Σωτὴρ, as he was called, a title also given to Janus of Delphi; and IASO, the daughter of Asclepios was the goddess of healing, under whose patronage were all the candidates for initiation in her father's temple,

---

and the name of *Chrestos* used as a title during the mysteries. It is mentioned in the *Iliad*, ii, 520, as "Chrisa" (χρῖσα.) Dr. Clarke suspected its ruins under the present site of *Krestona*, a small town, or village rather, in Phocis, near the Crissæan Bay. (See E. D. Clarke, 4th ed., Vol viii, p.239, "Delphi".)

[1] The root of χρητός (*Chretos*) and χρηστος (*Chrestos*) is one and the same; χράω, which means "consulting the oracle", in one sense, but in another one "consecrated", *set apart*, belonging to some temple, or oracle, or devoted to oracular services. On the other hand, the word χρε (χρέω) means "obligation", a "bond, duty", or one who is under the obligation of pledges or vows taken.

[2] The adjective χρηστὸς was also used as an adjective before proper names as a compliment, as in Plat. Theact. p. 166A, "Οὗτος ὁ Σωκράτης ὁ χρηστός"; "here Socrates is the *Chréstos*," and also as a surname, as shown by Plutarch (V. Phocion), who wonders how such a rough and dull fellow as Phocion could be surnamed *Chréstos*.

[3] There are strange features, quite suggestive, for an Occultist, in the myth (if one) of Janus. Some make of him the personification of *Kosmos*, others, of *Cælus* (heaven), hence he is "two-faced" because of his two characters of spirit and matter; and he is not only "Janus *Bifrons*" (two-faced), but also *Quadrifrons*—the perfect square, the emblem of the Kabbalistic Deity. His temples were built with *four* equal sides, with a door and *three* windows on each side. Mythologists explain it as an emblem of the *four* seasons of the year, and *three* months in each season, and in all of the twelve months of the year. During the mysteries of Initiation, however, he became the Day-Sun and the Night-Sun. Hence he is often represented with the number 300 in one hand, and in the other 65, or the number of days of the Solar year. Now *Chanoch* (Kanoch and *Enosh* in the Bible) is, as may be shown on Kabbalistic authority, whether son of Cain, son of Seth, or the son of Methuselah, one and the same personage. As *Chanoch* (according to Fuerst), "he is the *Initiator, Instructor—of* the astronomical circle and solar year," as son of Methuselah, who is said to have lived 363 years and been taken to heaven alive, as the representative of the Sun (or god). (See *Book of Enoch*). This patriarch has many features in common with Janus, who, exoterically, is Ion but IAO cabalistically, or Jehovah, the "Lord God of Generations," the mysterious Yodh, or ONE (a phallic number). For Janus or Ion is also *Consivius, a conserendo*, because he presided over generations. He is shown giving hospitality to Saturn (*Chronos* "time"), and is the *Initiator* of the year, or time divided into 365.

the novices or *chrestoi,* called "the sons of Iaso". (*Vide* for name, "Plutus", by Aristoph. 701.)

Now, if we remember, firstly, that the names of IESUS in their different forms, such as Iasius, Iasion, Jason, and Iasus, were very common in ancient Greece, especially among the descendants of Jasius (the Jasides), as also the number of the "sons of Iaso", the *Mystoï* and future Epoptai (Initiates), why should not the enigmatical words in the Sibylline Book be read in their legitimate light, one that had naught to do with a Christian prophecy? The secret doctrine teaches that the first two words ἸΗΣΟΥΣ ΧΡΕΙΣΤΟΣ mean simply "son of Iaso, a Chrestos", or servant of the oracular God. Indeed IASO (Ἰασώ) *is in the Ionic dialect IESO* (Ἰησώ), and the expression Ἰησοῦς *(Iesous)—in* its archaic form, ἸΗΣΟΥΣ— simply means "the son of Iaso or *Ieso",* the "healer", *i.e.,* ὁ Ἰησοῦς (υἱος). No objection, assuredly, can be taken to such rendering, or to the name being written *Ieso* instead of *Iaso,* since the first form is *Attic,* therefore incorrect, for the name is *Ionic.* "Ieso" from which "O' Iesous" (son of Ieso)—*i.e.,* a genitive, not a nominative—*is Ionic and cannot* be anything else, if the age of the Sibylline book is taken into consideration. Nor could the Sibyl of Erythrea have spelt it originally otherwise, as Erythrea, her very residence, was a town in Ionia (from Ion or Janus) opposite Chios; and that the *Ionic* preceded the *Attic* form.

Leaving aside in this case the mystical signification of the now famous Sibylline sentence, and giving its literal interpretation only, on the authority of all that has been said, the hitherto mysterious words would stand; "Son of LASO, CHRESTOS (the priest or servant) (of the) SON of (the) GOD (Apollo) the SAVIOR from the CROSS"—(of flesh or matter).[1] Truly, Christianity can never hope to be understood until every trace of dogmatism is swept away from it, and the dead letter sacrificed to the eternal Spirit of Truth, which is Horus, which is Crishna, which is Buddha, as much as it is the Gnostic Christos and the true Chist of Paul.

In the *Travels* of Dr. Clarke, the author describes a heathen monument found by him.

Within the sanctuary, behind the altar, we saw the fragments of a *marble cathedra,* upon the back of which we found the following inscription, exactly as it is here written, no part of it having been injured or obliterated, affording perhaps the only instance known of a sepulchral inscription upon a monument of this remarkable form.

The inscription ran thus: ΧΡΗΣΤΟΣ ΠΡΩΤΟΥ ΘΕΣΣΑΛΟΣ ΛΑΡΙΣΣΑΙΟΣ ΠΕΛΑΣΓΙΟΤΗΣ ΕΤΩΝ ΙΗ; or, "Chrestos, the first, a Thessalonian from Larissa, Pelasgiot, 18 years old Hero", Chrestos the first *(protou),* why? Read literally the inscription has little sense; interpreted esoterically, it is pregnant with meaning. As Dr. Clarke shows, the word Chrestos is found on the epitaphs of almost all the ancient Larissians; but it is preceded always by a proper name. Had the adjective Chrestos stood after a name, it would only mean "a good man", a posthumous compliment paid to the defunct, the same being often found on our own modern

---

[1] *Stauros* became the cross, the instrument of crucifixion, far later, when it began to be represented as a Christian symbol and with the Greek letter T, the Tau. *(Luc. Jud. Voc.)* Its primitive meaning was phallic, a symbol for the male and female elements; the great serpent of temptation, the body which had to be killed or subdued by the dragon of wisdom, the seven-vowelled solar chnouphis or Spirit of Christos of the Gnostics, or, again, Apollo killing Python.

tumular epitaphs. But the word Chrestos, standing alone and the other word, "protou", following it, gives it quite another meaning, especially when the deceased is specified as a "hero". To the mind of an Occultist, the defunct was a neophyte, who had died in his 18th year *of neophytism,*[1] and stood in the first or highest class of discipleship, having passed his preliminary trials as a "hero"; but had died before the last mystery, which would have made of him a "Christos", an *anointed,* one with the spirit of Christos or Truth in him. He had not reached the end of the "Way", though he had heroically conquered the horrors of the preliminary theurgic trials.

We are quite warranted in reading it in this manlier, after learning the place where Dr. Clarke discovered the tablet, which was, as Godfrey Higgins remarks, there, where "I should expect to find it, at Delphi, in the temple of the God IE.," who, with the Christians became Jah, or Jehovah, one with Christ Jesus. It was at the foot of Parnassus, in a gymnasium, "adjoining the Castalian fountain, which flowed by the ruins of Crisa, probably the town called Crestona", etc. And again. "In the first part of its course from the (Castalian) fountain, it (the river) separates the remains of the gymnasium . . . . from the valley of Castro", as it probably did from the old city of Delphi—the seat of the great oracle of Apollo, of the town of Krisa (or Kreusa) the great centre of initiations and of the *Chrestoi* of the decrees of the oracles, where the candidates for the last *labor* were anointed with the sacred oils[2] before being plunged into their last trance of forty-nine hours' duration (as to this day, in the East), from which they arose as glorified adepts or *Christoi."*

In the Clementine Recognitions it is announced that the father anointed his son with "oil that was taken from the wood of the Tree of Life, and from this anointing he is called the Christ": whence the Christian name. This again is Egyptian. Horus was the anointed son of the father. The mode of anointing him from the Tree of Life, portrayed on the monuments, is very primitive indeed; and the Horus of Egypt was continued in the Gnostic Christ, who is reproduced upon the Gnostic stones as the intermediate link betwixt the *Sorest* and the Christ, also as the Horus of both sexes. (*The Name and Nature of the Christ*—GERALD MASSEY.)

Mr. G. Massey connects the Greek Christos or Christ with the Egyptian *Karat,* the "mummy type of immortality", and proves it very thoroughly. He begins by saying that in Egyptian the "Word of Truth" is *Ma-Kheru,* and that it is the title of Horus. Thus, as he shows, Horus preceded Christ as the Messenger of the Word of Truth, the Logos or the manifestor of the divine nature in humanity. In the same paper he writes as follows:—

The Gnosis had three phases—astronomical, spirtual, and doctrinal, and all three can be identified with the Christ of Egypt. In the astronomical phase the

---

[1] Even to this day in India, the candidate loses his name and, as also in Masonry, his age (monks and nuns also changing their Christian names at their taking the order or veil), and begins counting his years from the day be is accepted a chela and enters upon the cycle of initiations. Thus Saul was "a child of one year", when he began to reign, though a grown-up adult. Sees I Samuel ch. xiii. I, and Hebrew scrolls. about his initiation by Samuel.

[2] Demosthenes, *De Corona,* 313, declares that the candidates for intitiation into the Greek mysteries were anointed with oil. So they are now in India, even in the initiation into the *Yogi* mysteries—various ointments or unguents being used.

constellation Orion is called the *Sahu* or *mummy.* The soul of Horus was represented as rising from the dead and ascending to heaven in the stars of Orion. The mummy-image was the preserved one, the saved, therefore a portrait of the Savior, as a type of immortality. This was the figure of a dead man, which, as Plutarch and Herodotus tell us, was carried round at an Egyptian banquet, when the guests were invited to look on it and eat and drink and be happy, because, when they died, they would become what the image symbolized—that is, they also would be immortal! This type of immortality was called the *Karest,* or *Karust,* and it *was* the Egyptian Christ. To *Kares* means to embalm, anoint, to make the Mummy as a type of the eternal; and, when made, it was called the *Karest;* so that this is not merely a matter of name for name, the *Karest* for the *Christ.*

This image of the *Karest* was bound up in a woof without a seam, the proper vesture of the Christ! No matter what the length of the bandage might be, and some of the mummy-swathes have been unwound that were 1,000 yards in length, the woof was from beginning to end without a seam. . . . Now, this seamless robe of the Egyptian *Karest* is a very tell-tale type of the mystical Christ, who becomes historic in the Gospels as the wearer of a coat or chiton, made without a seam, which neither the Greek nor the Hebrew fully explains, but which is explained by the Egyptian *Ketu* for the woof, and by the seamless robe or swathing without seam that was made for eternal wear, and worn by the Mummy-Christ, the image of immortality in the tombs of Egypt.

Further, Jesus is put to death in accordance with the instructions given for making the *Karest.* Not a bone must be broken. The true *Karest* must be perfect in every member. "This is he who comes out sound; whom men know not is his name."

In the Gospels Jesus rises again with every member sound, like the perfectly-preserved *Karest,* to demonstrate the physical resurrection of the mummy. But, in the Egyptian original, the mummy transforms. The deceased says: "I am spiritualised. I am become a soul. I rise as a God." This transformation into the spiritual image, the *Ka,* has been omitted in the Gospel.

This spelling of the name as Chrest or Chrést in Latin is supremely important, because it enables me to prove the identity with the Egyptian *Karest* or *Karust,* the name of the Christ as the embalmed mummy, which was the image of the resurrection in Egyptian tombs, the type of immortality, the likeness of the Horus, who rose again and made the pathway out of the sepulchre for those who were his disciples or followers. *Moreover, this type of the Karest or Mummy-Christ is reproduced* in *the Catacombs of Rome.* No representation of the supposed historic resurrection of Jesus has been found on any of the early Christian monuments. But, instead of the missing fact, we find the scene of Lazarus being raised from the dead. This is depicted over and over again as the typical resurrection where there' is no real one! The scene is not exactly in accordance with the rising from the grave in the Gospel. It is purely Egyptian, and Lazarus is an Egyptian mummy! Thus Lazarus, in each representation, *is* the mummy-type of the resurrection; Lazarus is the Karest, who was the Egyptian Christ, and who is reproduced by Gnostic art in the Catacombs of Rome as a form of the Gnostic Christ, who *was not and could not become an historical character.*

Further, as the thing is Egyptian, it is probable that the name is derived from Egyptian. If so, Laz (equal to Ras) means to be raised up, while *aru* is the mummy

93

by name. With the Greek terminal *s* this becomes Lazarus. In the course of humanising the mythos the typical representation of the resurrection found in the tombs of Rome and Egypt would become the story of Lazarus being raised from the dead. This Karest type of the Christ in the Catacombs is not limited to Lazarus.

By means of the *Karest* type the Christ and the Christians can both be traced in the ancient tombs of Egypt. The mummy was made in this likeness of the Christ. It was the Christ by name, identical with the *Chrestoi* of the Greek Inscriptions. Thus the honored dead, who rose again as the followers of Horus-Makheru, the Word of Truth, are found to be the Christians *οἱ χρηστοί*, on the Egyptian monuments. *Ma-Kheru* is the term that is always applied to the faithful ones who win the crown of life and wear it at the festival which is designated "Come thou to me"—an invitation by Horns the Justifier to those who are the "Blessed ones of his father, Osiris"—they who, having made the Word of Truth the law of their lives, were the Justified—*οἱ χρηστοί*, the Christians on Earth.

In a fifth century representation of the Madonna and child from the cemetery of St. Valentinus, the new-born babe lying in a box or crib *is* also the *Karest,* or mummy-type, further identified as the divine babe of the solar mythos by the disk of the sun and the cross of the equinox at the back of the infant's head. Thus the child-Christ of the historic faith is born, and visibly begins in the *Karest* image of the dead Christ, which was the mummy-type of the resurrection in Egypt for thousands of years before the Christian era. This doubles the proof that the Christ of the Christian Catacombs was a survival of the *Karest* of Egypt.

Moreover, as Didron shows, there was a portrait of the Christ who had his body *painted red!*[1] It was a popular tradition that the Christ *was* of a red complexion. This, too, may be explained as a survival of the Mummy-Christ. It was an aboriginal mode of rendering things *tapu* by coloring them red. The dead corpse was coated with red ochre—a very primitive mode of making the mummy, or the anointed one. Thus the God Ptah tells Rameses II. that he has *"re-fashioned his flesh in vermilion".* This anointing with red ochre is called *Kura* by the Maori, who likewise made the Karest or Christ.

We see the mummy-image continued on another line of decent when we learn that among other pernicious heresies and deadly sins with which the Knights Templars were charged, was the impious custom of adoring a Mummy that had red eyes. Their Idol, called Baphomet, is also thought to have been a mummy. . . . . The Mummy was the earliest human image of the Christ.

I do not doubt that the ancient Roman festivals called the *Charistia* were connected in their origin with the *Karest* and the *Eucharist* as a celebration in honor of the names of their departed kith and kin, for whose sakes they became reconciled at the friendly gathering once a year. . . . It is here, then, we have to seek the essential connection between the Egyptian Christ, the Christians, and the Roman Catacombs. These Christian Mysteries, ignorantly explained to be inexplicable, can be explained by Gnosticism and Mythology, but in no other way. It is not that they are insoluble by human reason, as their incompetent, howsoever highly paid, expounders now-a-days pretend. That is but the puerile apology of the unqualified for their own helpless ignorance—they who have never been in possession of the gnosis or science of the Mysteries by which alone these things

[1] *Because he is ca.balistically the new Adam, the "celestial man", and Adam was made of red earth.*

can be explained in accordance with their natural genesis. In Egypt only can we read the matter to the root, or identify the origin of the Christ by nature and by name, to find at last that the Christ was the Mummy-type, and that our Christology is mummified *mythology.—(Agnostic Annual.)*

The above is an explanation on purely scientific evidence, but, perhaps, a little too *materialistic,* just because of that science, notwithstanding that the author is a well-known Spiritualist. Occultism pure and simple finds the same mystic elements in the Christian as in other faiths, though it rejects as emphatically its dogmatic and *historic* character. It is a fact that in the terms Ιησοῦς ὁ χριστος (see *Acts* v, 42, ix, 14; I Corinthians, iii, 17, *etc.),* the article *ὁ* designating *Christos,* proves it simply a surname, like that of Phocion, who is referred to as Φωκίων ὁ χρηστός (Plut. v). Still, the personage (Jesus) so addressed—whenever he lived—was a great Initiate and a "Son of God".

For, we say it again, the surname Christos is based on, and the story of the crucifixion derived from, events that preceded it. Everywhere, in India as in Egypt, in Chaldea as in Greece, all these legends were built upon one and the same primitive type; the voluntary sacrifice of the *logoï—the rays* of the one LOGOS, the direct manifested emanation from the One ever-concealed Infinite and Unknown—whose *rays* incarnated in mankind. They consented to *fall into matter,* and are, therefore, called the "Fallen Ones". This is one of those great mysteries which can hardly be touched upon in a magazine article, but shall be noticed in a separate work of mine, *The Secret Doctrine,* very fully.

Having said so much, a few more facts may be added to the etymology of the two terms. Χριστὸς being the verbal adjective in Greek of χρίω, "to be rubbed on", *as ointment* or salve, and the word being finally brought to mean "the Anointed One", in Christian theology; and *Kri,* in Sanskrit, the first syllable in the name of Krishna, meaning "to pour out, or rub over, to cover with"[1] among many other things, this may lead one as easily to make of Krishna, "the anointed one". Christian philologists try to limit the meaning of Krishna's name to its derivation from *Krish,* "black"; but if the analogy and comparison of the Sanskrit with the Greek roots contained in the names of Chrestos, Christos, and *C*hrishna, are analyzed more carefully, it will be found that they are all of the same origin.[2]

"In Bockh's *Christian Inscriptions,* numbering 1,287, there is no single instance of an earlier date than the third century, wherein the name is not written *Christ* or *Chreist."* (*The Name and Nature of the Christ,* by G. Massey, *The Agnostic Annual.*

Yet none of these names can be unriddled, as some Orientalists imagine, merely with the help of astronomy and the knowledge of zodiacal signs in

---

[1] Hence the memorialising of the doctrine during the MYSTERIES. The pure monad, the "god" incarnating and becoming *Chrestos,* or man, on his trial of life, a series of those trials led him to the *crucifixion of flesh,* and finally into the Christos condition.

[2] On the best authority the derivation of the Greek *Christos* is shown from the Sanskrit root *ghársh*= "rub"; thus: *ghársh-ā-mi-to,* "to rub", and ghársh-tá-s "flayed, sore". Moreover, Krish, which means in one sense to plough and make furrows, means also to cause pain, "to torture to torment", and ghrsh-tā-s "rubbing"—all these terms relating to Chrestos and Christos conditions. One has *to die in Chrestos, i. e.,* kill one's personality and its passions, to blot out every idea of separateness from one's "Father", the Divine Spirit in man; to become one with the eternal and absolute *Life* and *Light* (SAT) before one can reach the glorious state of *Christos,* the regenerated man, the man in spiritual freedom.

conjunction with phallic symbols. Because, while the sidereal symbols of the mystic characters or personificatians in *Puranas* or *Bible,* fulfil astronomical functions, their spiritual anti-types rule invisibly, but very effectively, the world. They exist as abstractions on the higher plane, as manifested ideas on the astral, and become males, females, and androgyne powers on this lower plane of ours. *Scorpio, as Chrestos-Meshiac,* and Leo, as *Christos-Messiah antedated* by far the Christian era in the trials and triumphs of Initiation during the Mysteries, Scorpio standing as symbol for the latter, Leo for the glorified triumph of the "sun" of truth. The mystic philosophy of the allegory is well understood by the author of the *Source of Measures;* who writes: "One (Chrestos) causing himself to go down into the pit (of Scorpio, or incarnation in the womb) for the salvation of the world; this was the Sun, shorn of his *golden rays,* and *crowned with blackened[1] ones* (symbolizing this loss) as the thorns; *the other* was the triumphant *Messiah,* mounted up to the *summit of the arch of heaven,* personated as the *Lion of the tribe of Judah,.* In both instances he had the Cross; once in humiliation (as the son of copulation), and once holding it in his control, as the law of creation, he being Jehovah"—in the scheme of the authors of dogmatic Christianity. For, as the same author shows further, John, Jesus, and even Apollonius of Tyana were but epitomizers of the history of the Sun "under differences of aspect or condition".[2] The explanation, he says, "is simple enough, when it is considered that the names *Jesus,* Hebrew רשׁ and Apollonius, or Apollo, are alike names of the *Sun in the heavens,* and, necessarily, the history of the one, as to his travels through *the signs,* with the personifications of his sufferings, triumphs and miracles, could be but the *history of the other,* where there was a wide-spread, common method of describing those travels by personification". The fact that the Secular Church was founded by Constantine, and that it was a part of his decree "that the venerable day of the *Sun* should be the day set apart for the worship of Jesus Christ as Sunday", shows that they knew well in that "Secular Church" "that the allegory rested upon an astronomical basis", as the author affirms. Yet, again, the circumstance that both *Purânas* and *Bible* are full of solar and astronomical allegories, does not militate against that other fact that all such scriptures in addition to these two are *closed*

---

[1] The Orientalists and Thologians are invited to read over and study the allegory of Viswakarman, the "Omnificent", the Vedic God, the architect of the world, who sacrificed himself *to himself* or the world, after having offered up all worlds, *which are himself,* in a "Serve Madha" (general sacrifice)—and ponder over it. In the Purânic allegory, his daughter *Yoga-siddha* "Spiritual consciousness", the wife of *Surya,* the Sun, complains to him of the too great effulgence of her husband; and Viswakarmâ, in his character of *Takshaka,* "wood cutter and carpenter", placing the Sun upon his lathe cuts away a part of his brightness. Surya looks, after this, crowned with dark thorns instead of rays, and becomes Vikarttana ("shorn of his rays"). All these names are terms which were used by the candidates when going through the trials of Initiation. The Hierophant-Initiator personated Viswakarman; the father, and the general *artificer* of the gods (the adepts on earth), and the candidate-Surya, the Sun, who had to kill all his fiery passions and wear the crown of thorns *while crucifying his body* before he could rise and be re-born into a new life as the glorified "Light of the World"—Christos. No Orientalist seems to have ever perceived the suggestive analogy, let alone to apply it!

[2] The author of the *Source of Measures* thinks that this "serves to explain why it has been that the *Life of Apollonius of Tyana,* by Philostratus has been so carefully kept back from translation and popular reading". Those who have studied it in the original have been forced to the comment that either the *"Life of Apollonius* has been taken from the New Testament, or that New Testament narratives have been taken from the *Life of Apollonius,* because of the manifest sameness of the *means of construction* of the narrative". (p. 160).

books to the scholars "having authority".(!) Nor does it affect that other truth, that all those systems are *not the work of mortal man,* nor are they his invention in their origin and basis.

Thus "Christos", under whatever name, means more than *Karest, a mummy,* or even the "anointed" and the *elect* of theology. Both of the latter apply to *Chréstos,* the man of sorrow and tribulation, in his physical, mental, and psychic conditions, and both relate to the Hebrew *Mashiac* (from whence Messiah) condition, as the word is etymologised[1] by Fuerst, and the author of *The Source of Measures,* p. 255. Christos is the crown of glory of the suffering Chréstos of the mysteries, as of the candidate to the final UNION, of whatever race and creed. To the true follower of the SPIRIT OF TRUTH, it matters little, therefore, whether Jesus, as man and Chrestos, lived during the era called Christian, or before, or never lived at all. The Adepts, who lived and died for humanity, have existed in many and all the ages, and many were the good and holy men in antiquity who bore the surname or title of Chrestos before Jesus of Nazareth, otherwise Jesus (or Jehoshua) Ben Pandira was born.[2] Therefore, one may be permitted to conclude, with good reason, that Jesus, or Jehoshua, was like Socrates, like Phocian, like Theodorus, and so many others surnamed *Chréstos, i.e.,* the "good, and excellent", the gentle, and the holy Initiate, who showed the "way" to the Christos condition, became himself "the Way" in the hearts of his enthusiastic admirers. The Christians, as all the "Hero-worshippers" have tried to throw into the background all the other Chréstoï, who have appeared to them as rivals of *their* Man-God. But if the voice of the MYSTERIES has become silent for many ages in the West, if Eleusis, Memphis, Antium, Delphi, and Crèsa have long ago been made the tombs of a Science once as colossal in the West as it is yet in the East, there are successors now being prepared for them. We are in 1887 and the nineteenth century is close to its death. The twentieth century has strange developments in store for humanity, and may even be the last of its name.

H. P. B.

---

[1] "The word שׁיח *shiac,* is in Hebrew the same word as a verbal, signifying *to go down into the pit.* As a noun, *place of thorns, pit.* The *hifil* participle of this word is משׁיח or Messiach, or the Greek *Messias, Christ,* and means "he who causes to go down into the pit" (or hell, in dogmatism). In esoteric philosophy, this going down *into the pit* has the most mysterious significance. The Spirit "Christos" or rather the "Logos" (*read* Logoï), is said to "go down into the pit", when it incarnates in flesh, is *born as a man.* After having robbed the *Elohim* (or gods) of their secret, the *pro-creating* "fire of life", the Angels of Light are shown cast down into the pit or abyss of matter, called *Hell,* or the bottomless pit, by the kind theologians. This, in Cosmogony and Anthropology. During the Mysteries, however, it is the *Chréstos, neophyte,* (as man), etc., who had to descend into the crypts of Initiation and trials; and finally, during the "Sleep of Siloam" or the final *trance* condition, during the hours of which the new Initiate has the last and final mysteries of being divulged to him. Hades, Schéol, or Patala, are all one. The same takes place in the East now, as took place 2,000 years ago in the west, during the MYSTERIES.

[2] Several classics bear testimony to this fact. Lucian, c. 16, says Φωκίων ὀχρηστὸς, and Φωκίων ὁ ἐπίκλην (λεδόμενος, surnamed χρηστὸς). In Phædr. p. 226 E, it is written, "you mean Theodorus the Chrestos". Τὸν χρηστὸν λεγεις Φεὸδωρον. Plutarch shows the same, and Χρῆστος—chrestus is the proper name (see the word in *Thesaur.* Steph.) of *an* orator and disciple of Herodes Atticus.

III

No one can be regarded as a Christian unless he professes, or is supposed to profess, belief in Jesus, by baptism, and in salvation, "through the blood of Christ". To be considered a good Christian, one has, as a *conditio sine quâ non,* to show faith in the dogmas expounded by the Church and to profess them; after which a man is at liberty to lead a private and public life on principles diametrically opposite to those expressed in the Sermon on the Mount. The chief point and that which is demanded of him is, that he should have—or *pretend to have*—a blind faith in, and veneration for, the ecclesiastical teachings of his special Church.

Faith is the key of Christendom,

saith Chaucer, and the penalty for lacking it is as clearly stated as words can make it, in St. Mark's Gospel, Chapter xvi, verse 16th: "He that believeth and is baptised shall be saved; but he that believeth not shall be damned".

It troubles the Church very little that the most careful search for these words in the oldest texts during the last centuries, remained fruitless; or, that the recent revision of the Bible led to a unanimous conviction in the truth-seeking and truth-loving scholars employed in that task, that no such *un-Christ*-like sentence was to be found, except in some of the latest, fraudulent texts. The good Christian people had assimilated the consoling words, and they had become the very pith and marrow of their charitable souls. To take away the hope of eternal damnation, for all others except themselves, from these chosen vessels of the God of Israel, was like taking their very life. The truth-loving and God-fearing revisers got scared; they left the forged passage (an interpolation of eleven verses, from the 9th to the 20th), and satisfied their consciences with a foot-note remark of a very equivocal character, one that would grace the work and do honor to the diplomatic faculties of the craftiest Jesuits. It tells the "believer" that:—

The two oldest Greek MSS. and some other authorities OMIT from verse 9 to the end. Some authorities *have a different ending* to the Gospel,[1]—

—and explains no further.

But the two "oldest Greek MSS". *omit* the verses *nolens volens,* as these *have never existed.* And the learned and truth-loving revisers know this better than any of us do; yet the wicked falsehood is printed at the very seat of Protestant Divinity, and it is allowed to go on, glaring into the faces of coming generations of students of theology and, hence, into those of their future parishioners. Neither can be, nor are they deceived by it, yet both *pretend* belief in the authenticity of the cruel words worthy of a *theological Satan.* And this Satan-Moloch is their own *God of infinite mercy and justice* in Heaven, and the incarnate symbol of love and charity on Earth—blended in one!

Truly mysterious are your paradoxical ways, oh—Churches of Christ!

I have no intention of repeating here stale arguments and logical *exposés* of the whole theological scheme; for all this has been done, over and over again, and in a most excellent way, by the ablest "Infidels" of England and America. But I may

---

[1] Vide "Gospel according to St. Mark", in the *revised* edition printed for the Universities of Oxford and Cambridge, 1881.

briefly repeat a prophecy which is a self-evident result of the present state of men's minds in Christendom. Belief in the Bible *literally,* and in a *carnalized* Christ, will not last a quarter of a century longer. The Churches will have to part with their cherished dogmas, or the 20th century will witness the downfall and ruin of all Christendom, and with it, belief even in a Christos as pure Spirit. The very name has now become obnoxious, and theological Christianity must die out, *never to resurrect again in* its present form. This, in itself, would be the happiest solution of all, were there no danger from the natural reaction which is sure to follow: crass materialism will be the consequence and the result of centuries of blind faith, unless the loss of old ideals is replaced by other ideals, unassailable, because *universal,* and built on the rock of eternal truths instead of the shifting sands of human fancy. Pure immateriality must replace, in the end, the terrible anthropomorphism of those ideals in the conceptions of our modern dogmatists. Otherwise, why should Christian dogmas—the perfect counterpart of those belonging to other exoteric and pagan religions—claim any superiority? The bodies of all these were built upon the same astronomical and physiological (or phallic) symbols. Astrologically, every religious dogma the world over, may be traced to, and located in, the Zodiacal signs and the Sun. And so long as the science of comparative symbology or any theology has only two keys to open the mysteries of religious dogmas—and these two only very partially mastered, how can a line of demarcation be drawn, or any difference made between the religions of say, Chrishna and Christ, between salvation through the blood of the "first-born primeval male" of one faith, and that of the "only *begotten* Son" of the other, far younger, religion?

Study the *Vedas;* read even the superficial, often disfigured writings of our great Orientalists, and think over what you will have learnt. Behold Brahmans, Egyptian Hierophants, and Chaldean Magi, teaching several thousand years before our era that the gods themselves had been only mortals (in previous births) until they won their immortality by *offering their blood to their Supreme God* or chief. The *Book of the Dead* teaches that mortal man "became one with the gods through an interflow of a common life in the common blood of the two". Mortals gave the blood of their first-born sons in sacrifice to the Gods. In his *Hinduism,* p. 35, Professor Monier Williams, translating from the *Taitiriya Brâhmana,* writes:— "By means of the sacrifice the gods obtained heaven". And in the *Tandya Brâhmana:—"The* lord of creatures offered himself a sacrifice for the gods". . . . And again in the *Satapatha Brâhmana:—*"He who, knowing this, sacrifices with the *Purusha-madha* or the sacrifice of the primeval male, becomes everything".

Whenever I hear the Vedic rites discussed and called "disgusting human sacrifices", and cannibalism *(sic.),* I feel always inclined to ask, where's the difference? Yet there is one, in fact; for while Christians are compelled to accept the allegorical (though, when understood, highly philosophical) drama of the New Testament Crucifixion, as that of Abraham and Isaac literally,[1] Brahmanism—its philosophical schools at any rate—teaches its adherents, that this *(pagan) sacrifice* of the "primeval male" is a purely allegorical and philosophical symbol. Read in their dead-letter meaning, the four gospels are simply slightly altered versions of

[1] *Vide The Soldier's Daughter, Lucifer,* vol. I, No. 6, by the Rev. T. G. Headley, and notice the desperate protest of this *true* Christian, against the *literal* acceptance of the "blood sacrifices", "atonement by blood", etc., in the Church of England. The reaction begins: another *sign of the times.*

what the Church proclaims as Satanic plagiarisms (by anticipation) of Christian dogmas in Pagan religions. Materialism has a perfect right to find in all of them the same sensual worship and "solar" myths as anywhere else.

Analysed and critised superficially and on its dead-letter face, Professor Joly *(Man before Metals,* pp. 189-190) finding in the *Swastika,* the *crux ansata,* and the cross pure and simple, mere sexual symbols—is justified in speaking as he does. Seeing that "the father of the sacred fire (in India) bore the name of *Twaslitri,* that is the divine carpenter who made the *Swastika* and the *Pramantlla,* whose friction produced the divine child *Agni, in Latin Ignis;* that his mother was named *Maya;* he himself, styled *Akta (anointed,* or *Christos)* after the priests had poured upon his head the spirituous *soma* and on his body butter purified by sacrifice"; seeing all this he has a full right to remark that:—

The close resemblance which exists between certain ceremonies of the worship of *Agni* and certain rites of the Catholic religion may be explained by their common origin. *Agni* in the condition of *Akta,* or anointed, is suggestive of Christ; *Maya,* Mary, his mother; *Twashtri,* St. Joseph, the carpenter of the Bible.

Has the professor of the Science Faculty of Toulouse explained anything by drawing attention to that which anyone can see? Of course not. But if, in his ignorance of the esoteric meaning of the allegory he has added nothing to human knowledge, he has on the other hand destroyed faith in many of his pupils in both the *"divine* origin" of Christianity and its Church and helped to increase the number of Materialists. For surely, no man, once he devotes himself to such comparative studies, can regard the religion of the West in any light but that of a pale and enfeebled copy of older and nobler philosophies.

The origin of all religions—Judæo-Christianity included—is to be found in a few primeval truths, not one of which can be explained apart from all the others, as each is a complement of the rest in some one detail. And they are all, more or less, broken rays of the same Sun of truth, and their beginnings have to be sought in the archaic records of the Wisdom-religion. Without the light of the latter, the greatest scholars can see but the skeletons thereof covered with masks of fancy, and based mostly on personified Zodiacal signs.

A thick film of allegory and *blinds,* the "dark sayings" of fiction and parable, thus covers the original esoteric texts from which the New Testament—*as now known*—*was* compiled. Whence, then, the Gospels, the life of Jesus of Nazareth? Has it not been repeatedly stated that no human, *mortal* brain could have invented the life of the Jewish Reformer, followed by the awful drama on Calvary? We say, on the authority of the esoteric Eastern School, that all this came from the Gnostics, as far as the name Christos and the astronomico-mystical allegories are concerned, and from the writings of the ancient *Tanaïm* as regards the Kabalistic connection of Jesus or Joshua, with the Biblical personifications. One of these is the mystic esoteric name of Jehovah—not the present fanciful God of the profane Jews ignorant of their own mysteries, the God accepted by the still more ignorant Christians—but the compound Jehovah of the pagan Initiation. This is proven very plainly by the glyphs or mystic combinations of various signs which have survived to this day in the Roman Catholic hieroglyphics.

The Gnostic Records contained the epitome of the chief scenes enacted during the mysteries of Initiation, since the memory of man; though even that was given out invariably under the garb of semi-allegory, whenever entrusted to parchment or paper. But the ancient Tanaïm, the Initiates from whom the wisdom of the Kabala *(oral tradition)* was obtained by the later Talmudists, had in their possession the secrets of the mystery language, and it is *in this language that the Gospels* were written.[1] Ile alone who has mastered the esoteric cypher of antiquity—the secret meaning of the numerals, a common property at one time of all nations—has the full proof of the genius which was displayed in the blending of the purely Egypto-Jewish, Old Testament allegories and names, and those of the pagan-Greek Gnostics, the most refined of all the mystics of that day. Bishop Newton proves it himself quite innocently, by showing that "St. Barnabas, the companion of St-Paul, in his epistle (ch. ix) discovers . . . the name of Jesus crucified in the number 318", namely, Barnabas finds it in the mystic Greek I H T—the *tau* being the glyph of the cross. On this, *a* Kabalist, the author of an unpublished MS. on the Key of Formation of the Mystery Language, observes:— "But this is but a play upon the Hebrew letters *Jodh, Chith,* and *Shin,* from whence the I H S as the monogram of Christ coming down to our day, and this reads as שׁחי or 381, the sum of the letters being 318 or the number of Abraham and his Satan, and of Joshua and his Amalek . . . also the number of Jacob and his antagonist . . . (Godfrey Higgins gives the authority for the number 608) . . . It is the number of Melchizedek's name, for the value of the last is 304 and Melchizedek was the priest of the most high God, without beginning nor ending of days". The solution and secret of Melchizedek are found in the fact that "in the ancient Pantheons the two planets which had existed from eternity *(æonic* eternity) and were eternal, were the Sun and the Moon, or Osiris and Isis, hence the terms of *without beginning nor ending of days.* 304 multiplied by two is 608. So also the numbers in the word Seth, who was a type of the year. There are a number of authorities for the number 888 as applying to the name of Jesus Christ, and as said this is in antagonism to the 666 of the Anti-Christ . . . . . The staple value in the name of Joshua was the number 365, the indication of the Solar year, while Jehovah delighted in being the indication of the Lunar year—and Jesus Christ was both Joshua and Jehovah in the Christian Pantheon . . ."

This is but an illustration to our point to prove that the Christian application of the compound name Jesus-Christ is all based on Gnostic and Eastern mysticism. It was only right and natural that Chroniclers like the initiated Gnostics, pledged to secresy, should veil or *cloak* the final meaning of their oldest and most sacred teachings. The right of the Church fathers to cover the whole with an epitheme of euhemerized fancy is rather more dubious.[2] The Gnostic Scribe and Chronicler deceived no one. Every Initiate into the Archaic gnosis—whether of the pre-Christian or post-Christian period—knew well the value of every word of the "mystery-language". For these Gnostics—the inspirers of primitive Christianity—

---

[1] Thus while the three Synoptics display a combination of the pagan Greek and Jewish symbologies the *Revelation* is written in the mystery language of the Tanaïm—the relic of Egyptian and Chaldean wisdom—and St. John's Gospel is purely Gnostic.

[2] "The claim of Christianity to possess Divine authority rests on the ignorant belief that the mystical Christ could and did become a Person, whereas the gnosis proves the corporeal Christ to be only a counterfeit presentment of the trans-corporeal man; consequently, historical portraiture is, and ever must be, a fatal mode of falsifying and discrediting the Spiritual Reality." (G. Massey, *Gnostic and Historic Christianity.)*

were "the most cultured, the most learned and most wealthy of the Christian name", as Gibbon has it. Neither they, nor their humbler followers, were in danger of accepting the dead letter of their own texts. But it was different with the victims of the fabricators of what is now called *orthodox* and *historic* Christianity. Their successors have all been made to fall into the mistakes of the "foolish Galatians" reproved by Paul, who, as he tells them (Galat. iii, 1-5), having begun (by believing) in the Spirit (of Christos), "ended by believing in *the flesh*",—*i.e.*, a *corporeal* Christ. For such is the true meaning of the Greek sentence,[1] "*ἐναρξάμενοι Πνεύματι νῦν σαρκι ἐπιτελεῖσθε*". That Paul was *a* gnostic, a founder of a new sect of *gnosis* which recognized, as all other gnostic sects did, a "Christ-Spirit", though it went against its opponents, the rival sects, is sufficiently clear to all but dogmatists and theologians. Nor is it less clear that the primitive teachings of Jesus, whenever he may have lived, could be discovered only in Gnostic teachings; against which discovery, the falsifiers who dragged down Spirit into matter, thus degrading the noble philosophy of primeval Wisdom-Religion, have taken ample precautions from the first. The works of Basilides alone—"The philosopher devoted to the contemplation of Divine things", as Clement describes him—the 24 volumes of his *Interpretations upon the Gospels*—were all burned by order of the Church, Eusebius tells us (H. E., iv, 7).

As these *Interpretations* were written at *a* time when the Gospels we have now, were not yet in existence,[2] here is a good proof that the Evangel, the doctrines of which were delivered to Basilides by the Apostle Matthew, and Glaucus, the disciple of Peter (*Clemens Al. "Strom"*. vii. 7, § 106), must have differed widely from the present New Testament. Nor can these doctrines be judged by the distorted accounts of them left to posterity by Tertullian. Yet even the little this partisan fanatic gives, shows the chief gnostic doctrines to be identical, under their own peculiar terminology and personations, with those of the *Secret Doctrine* of the East. For, discussing Basilides, the "pious, god-like, theosophic philosopher", as Clement of Alexandria though him, Tertullian exclaims:—

After this, Basilides, the *Heretic,* broke loose.[3] He asserted that there is a Supreme God, by name Abraxas, by whom Mind (*Mahat*) was created, which the Greeks call *Nous*. From this emanated the Word; from the Word, Providence; from Providence, Virtue and Wisdom; from these two again, Virtues, *Principalities,*[4] *and Powers* were made; thence infinite productions and emissions of angels. Among the lowest angels, indeed, and those that made this world, he sets *last of all* the god of the Jews, whom he denies to be God himself, affirming that he is but

---

[1] This sentence analyzed means "Shall you, who in the beginning looked to the *Christ-Spirit,* now *end by* believing in a Christ of flesh", or it means nothing. The verb *ἐπιτελοῦμαι* has not the meaning of "becoming perfect", but of "ending by", becoming so. Paul's lifelong struggle with Peter and others, and what he himself tells of his vision of a Spiritual Christ and not of Jesus of Nazareth, as In the *Acts—are* so many proofs of this.

[2] see *Supernatural Religion,* vol. ii., chap. *Basilides.*

[3] It was asked in *Isis Unveiled,* were not the views of the Phrygian Bishop Montanus, also deemed a HERESY by the Church *of* Rome? It is quite extraordinary to see how easily that Church encourages the abuse of one *heretic,* Tertullian, against another *heretic,* Basilides, when the abuse happens to further her own object.

[4] Does not Paul himself speak of *"Principalities* and *Powers* in heavenly places" (EphesIans iii, 10; 1, 21), and confess that there be *gods* many and *Lords* many (Kurioi)? And angels, powers (Dunameis), and *Principalities?* (See I Corinthians, viii, 5; and Epistle to Romans, viii, 38.)

one of the angels.[1] (*Isis Unveiled,* vol. ii.)

Another proof of the claim that the Gospel of Matthew in the usual Greek texts is not the original gospel written in Hebrew, is given by no less an authority than St. Jerome (or Hieronymus). The suspicion of a conscious and gradual *euhemerization* of the Christ principle ever since the beginning, grows into a conviction, once that one becomes acquainted with a certain confession contained in book ii of the *Comment. to Matthew* by Hieronymus. For we find in it the proofs of a deliberate substitution of the whole gospel, the one now in the Canon having been evidently re-written by this too zealous Church Father.[2] He says that he was sent toward the close of the fourth century by "their Felicities", the Bishops Chromatius and Heliodorus to Cæsarea, with the mission to compare the Greek text (the only one they ever had) with the Hebrew original version preserved by the Nazarenes in their library, and to translate it. He translated it, but under protest; for, as he says, the *Evangel* "exhibited matter *not for edification, but for destruction.*[3] The "destruction" of what? Of the dogma that Jesus of Nazareth and the *Christos* are one—evidently; hence for the "destruction" of the newly planned religion.[4] In this same letter the Saint (who advised his converts to kill their fathers, trample on the bosom that fed them, by walking over the bodies of their mothers, if the parents stood as an obstacle between their sons and Christ)—admits that Matthew did not wish his gospel to be *openly written,* hence that the MS, *was a secret* one. But while admitting also that this gospel "was written in Hebrew characters and *by the hand of himself"(Matthew),* yet in another place he contradicts himself and assures posterity that *as it was tampered with, and re-written by a disciple of Manicheus, named Seleucus. . . .* "the ears of the Church properly refused to listen to it". *Hieronymus, Comment. to Matthew,* book ii chapter xii, 13).

No wonder that the very meaning of the terms *Chrestos* and *Christos,* and the bearing of both on "Jesus of Nazareth", a name coined out of Joshua the *Nazar,* has now become a dead letter for all with the exception of non-Christian Occultists. For even the Kabalists have no original data now to rely upon. The *Zohar* and the Kabala have been remodelled by Christian hands out of recognition; and were it not for a copy of the Chaldean *Book of Numbers* there would remain no better than garbled accounts. Let not our Brothers, the so-called Christian Kabalists of England and France, many of whom are Theosophists, protest too vehemently; for *this is history* (See Munk). It is as foolish to maintain, as some German Orientalists and modern critics still do, that the Kabala has never existed

---

[1] Tertullian: *Præscript,* It is undeniably owing only to a remarkably casuistical, sleight-of-hand-like argument that Jehovah, who in the *Kabala* is simply a Sephiroth, the third, left-hand power among the Emanations (Binah), has *been* elevated to the dignity of the *One* absolute God. Even in the Bible he is but one of the *Elohim* (see Genesis, chapter iii. v, 22, "The Lord God" making no difference between himself and others).

[2] This is *history.* How far that *re-writing* of, and tampering with, the primitive gnostic fragments which are now become the New Testament, went, may be inferred by reading *Supernatural Religion,* which went through over twenty-three editions, if I mistake not. The host of authorities for it given by the author, is simply appalling. The list of the English and German Bible critics alone seems endless.

[3] The chief details are given in *Isis Unveiled,* vol. ii, pp. 180-183, *et seq.* Truly faith in the infallibility of the Church must be *stone-blind*—or it could not have failed being killed and—dying.

[4] See Hieronymus: *De Viros,* illust cap. 3; Olshausen, *Neuen Test.,* p. 32. The Greek text of Matthew's Gospel is the only one used or ever possessed by the Church.

before the day of the Spanish Jew, Moses de Leon, accused of having forged this pseudograph in the 13th century, as to claim that any of the Kabalistical works now in our possession are as original as they were when Rabbi Simeon Ben Jochaï delivered the "traditions" to his son and followers. Not a single of these books is immaculate, none has escaped mutilation by Christian hands. Munk, one of the most learned and able critics of his day on this subject, proves it, while protesting as we do, against the assumption that it is a post-Christian forgery, for he says:—

"It appears evident to us that the author made use of ancient documents, and among these of certain *Midraschim* or collections of traditions and Biblical expositions, which we do not now possess."

After which, quoting from Tholuck (l. c. pp. 24 and 31), he adds:—

"Haya Gaon, who died in 1038, is to our knowledge the first author who developed the theory of the Sephiroth and he gave to them the names which we find again to be among the Kabalists (Tellenik, Moses ben Schem Tob di Leon, p. 13, note 5); this doctor, *who had intimate intercourse with the Syrian and Chaldean Christian savans,* was enabled by these last to acquire a knowledge of some of the Gnostic writings."

Which "Gnostic writings" and esoteric tenets passed part and parcel into the Kabalistic works, with many more modern interpolations that we now find in the *Zohar,* as Munk well proves. The Kabala is Christian now, not Jewish.

Thus, what with several generations of most active Church Fathers ever working at the destruction of old documents and the preparation of new passages to be interpolated in those which happen to survive, there remains of the *Gnostics*—the legitimate offspring of the Archaic Wisdom-religion—but a few unrecognisable shreds. But a particle of genuine gold will glitter for ever; and, however garbled the accounts left by Tertullian and Epiphanius of the Doctrines of the "Heretics", an occultist can yet find even in them traces of those primeval truths which were once universally imparted during the mysteries of Initiation. Among other works with most suggestive allegories in them, we have still the so-called *Apocryphal Gospels,* and the last discovered as the most precious relic of Gnostic literature, a fragment called *Pistis-Sophia,* "Knowledge-Wisdom".

In my next article upon the Esoteric character of the Gospels, I hope to be able to demonstrate that those who translate *Pistis by "Faith",* are utterly wrong. The word "faith" as *grace* or something to be believed in through unreasoned or blind faith, is a word that dates only since Christianity. Nor has Paul ever used this term in this sense in his Epistles; and Paul was undeniably—an INITIATE.

H. P. B.

(Was never finished.)

STUDIES IN OCCULTISM

A Series of Reprints from the Writings

of

H. P. BLAVATSKY

NO. VI

ASTRAL BODIES

CONSTITUTION OF THE INNER MAN

ASTRAL, BODIES,
OR DOPPELGÄNGERS

M.C. Great confusion exists in the minds of people about the various kinds of apparitions, wraiths, ghosts, or spirits. Ought we not to explain once for all the meaning of these terms? You say there are various kinds of "doubles"—what are they?

H. P. B. Our occult philosophy teaches us that there are three kinds of "doubles," to use the word in its widest sense. First, man has his "double" or *shadow*, properly so called, around which the physical body of the *fetus*—the future man—is built. The imagination of the mother, or an accident which affects the child, will affect also the astral body. The astral and the physical both exist before the mind is developed into action, and before the *Âtmâ* awakes. This occurs when the child is seven years old, and with it comes the responsibility attaching to a conscious sentient being. This "double" is born with man, dies with him, and can never separate itself far from the body during life, and though surviving him, it disintegrates, *pari passu,* with the corpse. It is this which is sometimes seen over the graves like a luminous figure of the man that was, during certain atmospheric conditions. From its physical aspect it is, during life, *man's vital* double, and after death, only the gases given off from the decaying body. But, as regards its origin and essence, it is something more. This double is what we have agreed to call *Linga-śarîra,* but which I would propose to call, for greater convenience, "Protean" or "Plastic Body."

M. C. Why Protean or Plastic?

H. P. B. Protean, because it can assume all forms; e. g., the "shepherd magicians" whom popular rumor accuses, perhaps not without some reason, of being "were-wolves," and "mediums in cabinets," whose own "Plastic Bodies" play the part of materialized grandmothers and "John Kings." Otherwise, why the invariable custom of the "dear departed angels" to come out but little further than arm's length from the medium, whether entranced or not? Mind, I do not at all deny foreign influences in this kind of phenomena. But I do affirm that foreign interference is rare, and that the materialized form is always that of the medium's *Astral,* or Protean body.

M. C. How is this astral body created?

H. P. B. It is not created; it grows, as I told you, with the man and exists in the rudimentary condition even before the child is born.

M. C. And what about the second?

H. P. B. The second is the "Thought" body, or Dream body, rather; known among Occultists as the *Mâyâvi-rûpa,* or "Illusion-body." During life this image is the vehicle both of thought and of the animal passions and desires, drawing at one and the same time from the lowest terrestrial *mamas* (mind) and *Kâma,* the element of desire. It is dual in its potentiality, and after death forms what is called in the East *Bhût,* or *Kâma-rûpa,* but which is better known to Theosophists as the "Spook."

M. C. And the third?

H. P. B. The third is the true *Ego,* called in the East by a name meaning "causal-body," but which in the *trans*-Himâlayan schools is always called the

"Karmic body," which is the same. For *Karma*, or action, is the cause which produces incessant rebirths or "reincarnations." It is *not* the *Monad*, nor is it *Manas* proper; but is, in a way, indissolubly connected with and a compound of the Monad and Manas in Devachan.

M. C. Then there are three doubles?

H. P. B. If you call the Christian and other Trinities "three Gods," then there are three doubles. But in truth there is only one under three aspects or phases: the most material portion disappearing with the body; the middle one surviving both as an independent but temporary entity in the land of shadows; the third, immortal throughout the Manvantara, unless Nirvâna puts an end to it before.

M. C. But shall not we be asked what difference there is between the *Mâyâvi* and *Kâma-rûpa,* or as you propose to call them the "Dream body" and the "Spook"?

H. P. B. Most likely, and we shall answer, in addition to what has been said, that the "thought-power" or aspect of the *Mâyâvi* or "Illusion-body," merges after death entirely into the causal body or the conscious, *thinking* Ego. The animal elements, or power of desire of the "Dream body," absorbing after death that which it has collected (through its insatiable desire *to live*) during life; *i.e.,* all the astral vitality as well as all the impressions of its *material* acts and thoughts while it lived in possession of the body, forms the "Spook" or *Kâma-rûpa.* Our Theosophists know well enough that after death the *higher* Manas unites with the *Monad* and passes into Devachan, while the dregs of the *lower* Manas or animal mind go to form this Spook. This has life in it, but hardly any consciousness, except, as it were, by proxy; when it is drawn into the current of a medium.

M. C. Is it all that can be said upon the subject?

H. P. B. For the present this is enough metaphysics, I guess. Let us hold to the "Double" in its earthly phase. What would you know?

M. C. Every country in the world believes more or less in the "double" or doppelgänger. The simplest form of this is the appearance of a man's phantom the moment after his death, or at the instant of death, to his dearest friend. Is this appearance the *mâyâvi-rûpa?*

H. P. B. It is; because produced by the thought of the dying man.

M. C. Is it unconscious?

H. P. B. It is unconscious to the extent that the dying man does not generally do it knowingly; nor is he aware that he so appears. What happens is this. If he thinks very intently at the moment of death of the person he either is very anxious to see, or loves best, he may appear to that person. The thought becomes objective; the double, or shadow of a man, being nothing but the faithful reproduction of him, like a reflection in a mirror: that which the man does, even in thought, that the double repeats. This is why the phantoms are often seen in such cases in the clothes they wear at the particular moment, and the *image* reproduces even the expression on the dying man's face. If the double of a man bathing were seen it would seem to be immersed in water; so when a man who has been drowned appears to his friend, the image will be seen to be dripping with water. The cause for the apparition may also be reversed; *i. e.,* the dying man may or may not be thinking at all of the particular person his image appears to, but it is that person who is sensitive. Or perhaps his sympathy or his hatred for the individual whose wraith is thus evoked is very intense physically or psychically; and in this case the apparition is created by, and depends upon the intensity of the thought. What then happens is this. Let us call the dying man A, and him who sees the double B. The latter, owing to love, hate, or fear, has the image of A so deeply impressed on his psychic memory, that actual magnetic attraction and repulsion are established between the two, whether one knows of it and feels it, or not. When A dies, the sixth sense or psychic spiritual intelligence of the *inner man* in B becomes cognizant of the change in A, and forthwith apprizes the physical senses of the man by projecting before his eye the form of A as it is at the instant of the great change. The same when the dying man longs to see some one; *his* thought telegraphs to his friend, consciously or unconsciously along the wire of sympathy, and becomes objective. This is what the "Spookical" Research Society would pompously, but none the less muddily call *telepathetic impact.*

M. C. This applies to the simplest form of the appearance of the double. What about cases in which the double does that which is contrary to the feeling and wish of the man?

H. P. B. This is impossible. The "Double" cannot act unless the key-note of this action was struck in the brain of the man to whom the "Double" belongs, be that man just dead, or alive, in good or in bad health. If he paused on the thought a second, long enough to give it form, before he passed on to other mental pictures, this one second is as sufficient for the *objectivization* of his personality on the astral waves, as for your face to impress itself on the sensitized plate of a photographic apparatus. Nothing prevents your form then being seized upon by the surrounding Forces—as a dry leaf fallen from a tree is taken up and carried away by the wind—being made to caricature or distort your thought.

M. C. Supposing the double expresses in actual words a thought uncongenial to the man, and expresses it—let us say to a friend far away, perhaps on another continent? I have known instances of this occurring.

H. P. B. Because it then so happens that the created image is taken up and used by a "Shell." Just as in séance-rooms when "images" of the dead—which may perhaps be lingering unconsciously in the memory or even the auras of those present—are seized upon by the Elementals or Elementary Shadows and made objective to the audience, and even caused to act at the bidding of the strongest of the many different wills in the room. In your case, moreover, there must exist a connecting link a—telegraph wire—between the two persons, a point of psychic sympathy, and on this the thought travels instantly. Of course there must be, in every case, some strong reason why that particular thought takes that direction; it must be connected in some way with the other person. Otherwise such apparitions would be of common and daily occurrence.

M. C. This seems very simple; why then does it only occur with exceptional persons?

H. P. B. Because the plastic power of the imagination is much stronger in some persons than in others. The mind is dual in its potentiality: it is physical and metaphysical. The higher part of the mind is connected with the spiritual soul or Buddhi, the lower with the animal soul, the Kâma principle. There are persons who never think with the higher faculties of their minds at all; those who do so are the minority and are thus, in a way, *beyond*, if not above, the average of human kind. These will think even upon ordinary matters on that *higher* plane. The idiosyncrasy of the person determines in which "principle" of the mind the thinking is done, as also the faculties of a preceding life, and sometimes the heredity of the physical. This is why it is so very difficult for a materialist—the metaphysical portion of whose brain is almost atrophied—to raise himself, or for one who is naturally spiritually-minded to descend to the level of the matter-of-fact vulgar thought. Optimism and pessimism depend on it also in a great measure.

M. C. But the habit of thinking in the higher mind can be developed—else there would be no hope for persons who wish to alter their lives and raise themselves? And that this is possible must be true, or there would be no hope for the world.

H. P. B. Certainly it can be developed, but only with great difficulty, a firm determination, and through much self-sacrifice. But it is comparatively easy for those who are born with the gift. Why is it that one person sees poetry in a cabbage or a pig with her little ones, while another will perceive in the loftiest things only their lowest and most material aspect, will laugh at the "music of the spheres," and ridicule the most sublime conceptions and philosophies? This difference depends simply on the innate power of the mind to think on the higher or on the lower plane, with the *astral* (in the sense given to the word by St. Martin), or with the physical brain. Great intellectual powers are often no proof of, but are impediments to spiritual and right conceptions; witness most of the great men of science. We must rather pity than blame them.

M. C. But how is it that the person who thinks on the higher plane produces more perfect and more potential images and objective forms by his thought?

H. P. B. Not necessarily that "person" alone, but all those who are generally sensitives. The person who is endowed with this faculty of thinking about even the most trifling things from the higher plane of thought has, by virtue of that gift which he possesses, a plastic power of formation, so to say, in his very imagination. Whatever such a person may think about, his thought will be so far more intense than the thought of an ordinary person, that by this very intensity it obtains the power of creation. Science has established the fact that thought is an energy. This energy in its action disturbs the atoms of the astral atmosphere around us. I already told you; the rays of thought have the same potentiality for producing forms in the astral atmosphere as the sunrays have with regard to a lens. Every thought so evolved with energy from the brain, creates, *nolens volens* a shape.

M. C. Is that shape absolutely unconscious?

H. P. B. Perfectly unconscious unless it is the creation of an adept, who has a preconceived object in giving it consciousness, or rather in sending along with it enough of his will and intelligence to cause it to appear conscious. This ought to make us more cautious about our thoughts.

But the wide distinction that obtains between the adept in this matter and the ordinary man must be borne in mind. The adept may at his will use his *Mâyâvi-rûpa*, but the ordinary man does not, except in very rare cases. It is called *Mâyâvi-rûpa* because it is a form of illusion created for use in the particular instance, and it has quite enough of the adept's mind in it to accomplish its purpose. The ordinary man merely creates a thought-image, whose properties and powers are at the time wholly unknown to him.

M. C. Then one may say that the form of an adept appearing at a distance from his body, as for instance Ram Lal in *Mr. Isaacs,* is simply an image?

H. P. B. Exactly. It is a walking thought.

M. C. In which case an adept can appear in several places almost simultaneously.

H. P. B. He can. Just as Apollonios of Tyana, who was seen in two places at once, while his body was at Rome. But it must be understood that not *all* of even the *astral* adept is present in each appearance.

M. C. Then it is very necessary for a person of any amount of imagination and psychic powers to attend to their thoughts?

H. P. B. Certainly, for each thought has a shape which borrows the appearance of the man engaged in the action of which he thought. Otherwise how can clairvoyants see in your *aura* your past and present? What they see is a passing panorama of yourself represented in successive actions by your thoughts. You asked me if we are punished for our thoughts. Not for all, for some are still-born; but for the others, those which we call "silent" but potential thoughts—yes. Take an extreme case, such as that of a person who is so wicked as to wish the death of another. Unless the evil-wisher is a *Dugpa,* a high adept in black magic, in which case Karma is delayed, such a wish only comes back to roost.

M. C. But supposing the evil-wisher to have a very strong will, without being a *dugpa,* could the death of the other be accomplished?

H. P. B. Only if the malicious person has the evil eye, which simply means possessing enormous plastic power of imagination working involuntarily, and thus turned unconsciously to bad uses. For what is the power of the "evil eye"? Simply a great plastic power of thought, so great as to produce a current impregnated with the potentiality of every kind of misfortune and accident, which inoculates, or attaches itself to any person who comes within it. A *jettatore* (one with the evil eye) need not be even imaginative, or have evil intentions or wishes. He may be simply a person who is naturally fond of witnessing or reading about sensational scenes, such as murder, executions, accidents, etc., etc. He may be not even thinking of any of these at the moment his eye meets his future victim. But the currents have been produced and exist in his visual ray ready to spring into activity the instant they find suitable soil, like a seed fallen by the way and ready to sprout at the first opportunity.

M. C. But how about the thoughts you call "silent"? Do such wishes or thoughts come home to roost?

H. P. B. They do; just as a ball which fails to penetrate an object rebounds upon the thrower. This happens even to some *dugpas* or sorcerers who are not strong enough, or do not comply with the rules—for even they have *rules* they have to abide by—but not with those who are regular, fully developed "black magicians"; for such have the power to accomplish what they wish.

M. C. When you speak of rules it makes me want to wind up this talk by asking you what everybody wants to know who takes any interest in occultism. What is a principal or important suggestion for those who have these powers and wish to control them rightly—in fact to enter occultism?

H. P. B. The first and most important step in occultism is to learn how to adapt your thoughts and ideas to your plastic potency.

M. C. Why is this so important?

H. P. B. Because otherwise you are creating things by which you may be making bad Karma. No one should go into occultism or even touch it before he is perfectly acquainted with his own powers, and that he knows how to commensurate it with his actions. And this he can do only by deeply studying the philosophy of Occultism before entering upon the *practical* training. Otherwise, as sure as fate—HE WILL FALL INTO BLACK MAGIC.

CONSTITUTION OF THE
INNER MAN

M. OF course it is most difficult, and, as you say, "puzzling" to understand correctly and distinguish between the various *aspects,* called by us the "principles" of the real EGO. It is the more so as there exists a notable difference in the numbering of those principles by various Eastern schools, though at the bottom there is the same identical substratum of teaching in all of them.

X. Are you thinking of the Vedântins? They divide our seven "principles" into five only, I believe?

M. They do; but though I would not presume to dispute the point with a learned Vedâtin, I may yet state as my private opinion that they have an obvious reason for it. With them it is only that compound spiritual aggregate which consists of various mental aspects that is called *Man* at all, the physical body being in their view something beneath contempt, and merely an *illusion.* Nor is the Vedânta the only philosophy to reckon in this manner. Lao-Tze in his *Tao-te-King,* mentions only five principles, because he, like the Vedântins, omits to include two principles, namely, the spirit (Âtmâ) and the physical body, the latter of which, moreover, he calls "the cadaver." Then there is the *Târaka Râja Yoga* School. Its teaching recognizes only three "principles" in fact; but then, in reality, their *Sthûlopâdhi,* or the physical body in its *jâgrata* or waking conscious state, their *Sûkshmopâdhi,* the same body in *svapna* or the dreaming state, and their *Kâtranopâdhi* or "causal body," or that which passes from one incarnation to another, are all dual in their aspects, and thus make six. Add to this Âtmâ, the impersonal divine principle or the immortal element in Man, undistinguished from the Universal Spirit, and you have the same seven, again, as in the esoteric division.[1]

X. Then it seems almost the same as the division made by mystic Christians: body, soul, and spirit?

M. Just the same. We could easily make of the body the vehicle of the "vital Double"; of the latter the vehicle of Life or *Prâna;* of *Kâma-rûpa* or (animal) soul, the vehicle of the *higher* and the *lower* mind, and make of this six principles, crowning the whole with the one immortal spirit. In Occultism, every qualificative change in the state of our consciousness gives to man a new aspect, and if it prevails and becomes part of the living and acting EGO, it must be (and is) given a special name, to distinguish the man in that particular state from the man he is when he places himself in another state.

X. It is just that which is so difficult to understand.

M. It seems to me very easy, on the contrary, once that you have seized the main idea, *i. e.,* that man acts on this, or another plane of consciousness, in strict accordance with his mental and spiritual condition. But such is the materialism of the age that the more we explain, the less people seem capable of understanding what we say. Divide the terrestrial being called man into three chief aspects, if you like; but, unless you make of him a pure animal, you cannot do less. Take his objective *body;* the feeling principle in him—which is only a little higher than the

----

[1] See *The Secret Doctrine* for a clearer explanation.

instinctual element in the animal—or the vital elementary soul; and that which places him so immeasurably beyond and higher than the animal—*i.e.*, his *reasoning* soul or "spirit." Well, if we take these three groups or representatives entities, and subdivide them, according to the occult teaching, what do we get?

First of all Spirit (in the sense of the Absolute, and therefore invisible ALL) or Âtmâ. As this can neither be located nor conditioned in philosophy, being simply that which IS, in Eternity, and as the ALL cannot be absent from even the tiniest geometrical or mathematical point of the universe of matter or substance, it ought not to be called, in truth, a "human" principle at all. Rather, and at best, it is that point in metaphysical Space which the human Monad and its vehicle man, occupy for the period of every life. Now that point is as imaginary as man himself, and in reality is an illusion, a *mâyâ;* but then for ourselves as for other personal Egos, we are a reality during that fit of illusion called life, and we have to take ourselves into account—in our own fancy at any rate, if no one else does. To make it more conceivable to the human intellect, when first attempting the study of Occultism, and to solve the A B C of the mystery of man, Occultism calls it the *seventh* principle, the synthesis of the six, and gives it for vehicle the *Spiritual* Soul, *Buddhi.* Now the latter conceals a mystery, which is never given to any one with the exception of irrevocably pledged *chelas,* those at any rate, who can be safely trusted. Of course there would be less confusion, could it only be told; but, as this is directly concerned with the power of projecting one's double consciously and at will, and as this gift like the "ring of Gyges" might prove very fatal to men at large and to the possessor of that faculty in particular, it is carefully guarded. Alone the adepts, who have been tried and can never be found wanting, have the key of the mystery fully divulged to them. . . . Let us avoid side issues, however, and hold to the "principles." This divine soul or Buddhi, then, is the Vehicle of the Spirit. In conjunction, these two are one, impersonal, and without any attributes (on this plane, of course), and make two spiritual "principles." If we pass on to the *Human* Soul (*manas,* the *mens*) every one will agree that the intelligence of man is *dual* to say the least: e. g. the high-minded man can hardly become low-minded; the very intellectual and spiritual-minded man is separated by an abyss from the obtuse, dull and material, if not animal-minded man. Why then should not these men be represented by two "principles" or two aspects rather? Every man has these two principles in him, one more active than the other, and in rare cases, one of these is entirely stunted in its growth: so to say paralysed by the strength and predominence of the other *aspect,* during the life of man. These, then, are what we call the two principles or aspects of *Manas,* the higher and the lower; the former, the higher Manas, or the thinking, conscious Eco gravitating toward the Spiritual Soul (Buddhi); and the latter, or its instinctual principle attracted to *Kâma,* the seat of animal desires and passions in man. Thus, we have *four* "principles" justified; the last three being (1) the "Double" which we have agreed to call Protean, or Plastic Soul; the vehicle of (2) the life *principle;* and (3) the physical body. Of course no Physiologist or Biologist will accept these principles, nor can he make head or tail of them. And this is why, perhaps, none of them understand to this day either the functions of the spleen, the physical vehicle of the Protean Double, or those of a certain organ on the right side of man, the seat of the above mentioned desires, nor yet does he know anything of the pineal gland, which he describes as a horny gland with a little sand in it, and which is the very key to the highest and divinest consciousness in man—his omniscient, spiritual and all embracing mind. This seemingly useless appendage is the pendulum which, once the clockwork of the *inner* man is wound up, carries the spiritual vision of the EGO to the highest planes of perception, where the horizon open before it becomes almost infinite. . . .

X. But the scientific materialists assert that after the death of man nothing remains; that the human body simply disintegrates into its component elements, and that what we call soul is merely a temporary self-consciousness produced as a by-product of organic action, which will evaporate like steam. Is not theirs a strange state of mind?

M. Not strange at all, that I see. If they say that self-consciousness ceases with the body, then in *their* case they simply utter an unconscious prophecy. For once that they are firmly convinced of what they assert, no conscious after-life is possible for them.

X. But if human self-consciousness survives death as a rule, why should there be exceptions?

M. In the fundamental laws of the spiritual world which are immutable, no exception is possible. But there are rules for those who see, and rules for those who prefer to remain blind.

X. Quite so, I understand. It is an aberration of a blind man, who denies the existence of the sun because he does not see it. But after death his spiritual eyes will certainly compel him to see.

M. They will not compel him, nor will he see anything. Having persistently denied an after-life during this life, he will be unable to sense it. His spiritual senses having been stunted, they cannot develop after death, and he will remain blind. By insisting that he *must* see it, you evidently mean one thing and I another. You speak of the spirit from the Spirit, or the flame from the Flame—of Âtmâ in short—and you confuse it with the human soul—Manas. . . . You do not understand me, let me try to make it clear. The whole gist of your question is to know whether, in the case of a downright materialist, the complete loss of self-consciousness and self-perception after death is possible? Isn't it so? I say: It is possible. Because, believing firmly in our Esoteric Doctrine, which refers to the *post-mortem* period, or the interval between two lives or births as merely a transitory state, I say:—Whether that interval between two acts of the illusionary drama of life lasts one year or a million, that *post-mortem* state may, without any breach of the fundamental law, prove to be just the same state as that of a man who is in a dead swoon.

X. But since you have just said that the fundamental laws of the after-death state admit of no exceptions, how can this be?

M. Nor do I say now that they admit of exceptions. But the spiritual law of continuity applies only to things which are truly real. To one who has read and understood *Mândukya Upanishad* and *Vedânta-Sâra, all* this becomes very clear. I will say more: it is sufficient to understand what we mean by Buddhi and the duality of Manas to have a very clear perception why the materialist may not have a self-conscious survival after death: because Manas, in its lower aspect, is the seat of the terrestrial mind, and, therefore, can give only that perception of the Universe which is based on the evidence of that mind, and not on our spiritual vision. It is said in our Esoteric school that between Buddhi and Manas, or Îsvara and Prajñâ,[1] there is in reality no more difference than *between a forest and its trees, a lake and its waters,* just as *Mândukya* teaches. One or hundreds of trees dead from loss of vitality, or uprooted, are yet incapable of preventing the forest from being still a forest. The destruction or *post-mortem* death of one personality dropped out of the long series, will not cause the smallest change in the Spiritual *Ego,* and it will ever remain the same EGO. Only, instead of experiencing *Devachan* it will have to immediately reincarnate.

X. But as I understand it, Ego-Buddhi represents in this simile the forest and the personal minds the trees. And if Buddhi is immortal, how can that which is similar to it, *i.e., Manas-taijasi,*[2] lose entirely its consciousness till the day of its new incarnation? I cannot understand it.

M. You cannot, because you will mix up an abstract representation of the whole with its casual changes of form; and because you confuse *Manas-taijasi,* the *Buddhi*-lit human soul, with the latter, animalized. Remember that if it can be said of Buddhi that it is unconditionally immortal, the same cannot be said of *Manas,* still less of *taijasi,* which is an attribute. No *post-mortem* consciousness or Manas-taijaii, can exist apart from Buddhi, the divine soul, because the first (*Manas*) *is, in* its lower aspect, a qualificative attribute of the terrestrial personality, and the second (*taijasi*) is identical with the first, and that it is the same Manas only with the light of Buddhi reflected on it. In its turn, Buddhi would remain only an impersonal spirit without this element which it borrows from the human soul, which conditions and makes of it, in this illusive Universe, *as it were something separate* from the universal soul for the whole period of the cycle of incarnation. Say rather that *Buddhi-Manas* can neither die-nor lose its compound self-consciousness in Eternity, nor the recollection of its previous incarnations in which the two—*i. e.,* the spiritual and the human soul, had been closely linked together. But it is not so in the case of a materialist, whose human soul not only receives nothing from the divine soul, but even refuses to recognize its existence. You can hardly apply this axiom to the attributes and qualifications of the human soul; for it would be like saying that because your divine soul is immortal, therefore the bloom on your cheek must also be immortal; whereas this bloom, like *taijasi,* or spiritual radiance, is simply a transitory phenomenon.

X. Do I understand you to say that we must not mix in our minds the noumenon with the phenomenon, the cause with its effect?

M. I do say so, and repeat that, limited to Manas or the human soul alone, the radiance of Taijasi itself becomes a mere question of time; because both immortality and consciousness after death become for the terrestrial personality of man simply conditioned attributes, as they depend entirely on conditions and beliefs created by the human soul itself during the life of its body. Karma acts incessantly: we reap *in our after*-life only the fruit of that which we have ourselves sown, or rather created in our terrestrial existence.

---

[1] Îsvara is the collective consciousness of the manifested deity, Brahmâ, i. e., the collective consciousness of the Host of Dhyâni Chohans; and Prajñâ is their individual wisdom.

[2] *Taijasi* means the radiant in consequence of the union with Buddhi of Manas, the human, illuminated by the radiance of the divine soul. Therefore Manas-taijasi may be described as radiant mind; the *human* reason lit by the light of the spirit; and Buddhi-Manas is the representation of the divine *plus* the human intellect and self-consciousness.

X. But if my Ego can, after the destruction of my body, become plunged in a state of entire unconsciousness, then where can be the punishment for the sins of my past life?

M. Our philosophy teaches that Karmic punishment reaches the. Ego only in its next incarnation. After death it receives only the reward for the unmerited sufferings endured during its just past existence.[1] The whole punishment after death, even for the materialist, consists therefore in the absence of any reward and the utter loss of the consciousness of one's bliss and rest. Karma—is the child of the terrestrial Ego, the fruit of the actions of the tree which is the objective personality visible to all, as much as the fruit of all the thoughts and even motives of the spiritual "I"; but Karma is also the tender mother, who heals the wounds inflicted by her during the preceding life, before she will begin to torture this Ego by inflicting upon him new ones. If it may be said that there is not a mental or physical suffering in the life of a mortal, which is not the fruit and consequence of some sin in this, or a preceding existence, on the other hand, since he does not preserve the slightest recollection of it in his actual life, and feels himself not deserving of such punishment, but believes sincerely he suffers for no guilt of his own, this alone is quite sufficient to entitle the human soul to the fullest consolation, rest and bliss in his *post-mortem* existence. Death comes to our spiritual selves ever as a deliverer and friend. For the materialist, who, notwithstanding his materialism, was not a bad man, the interval between the two lives will be like the unbroken and placid sleep of a child; either entirely dreamless, or with pictures of which he will have no definite perception. For the believer it will be a dream as vivid as life and full of realistic bliss and visions. As for the bad and cruel man, whether materialist or otherwise, he will be immediately reborn and suffer his hell on earth. To enter *Avitchi is* an exceptional and rare occurrence.

X. As far as I remember, the periodical incarnations of Sûtrâtmâ[2] are likened in some Upanishad to the life of a mortal which oscillates periodically between sleep and waking. This does not seem to me very clear, and I will tell you why. For the man who awakes, another day commences, but that man is the same in soul and body as he was the day before; whereas at every new incarnation a full change takes place not only in his external envelop, sex and personality, but even in his mental and psychic capacities. Thus the simile does not seem to me quite correct. The man who arises from sleep remembers quite clearly what he has done yesterday, the day before, and even months and years ago. But none of us has the

---

[1] Some Theosophists have taken exception to this phrase, but the words are those of the Masters, and the meaning attached to the word "unmerited" is that given above. In the T. P. S. pamphlet No. 6 a phrase, criticised subsequently in *Lucifer,* was used, which was intended to convey the same idea. In form, however it was awkward and open to the criticism directed against it; but the essential idea was that men often suffer from the effects of the actions done by others, effects which thus do not strictly belong to their own Karma, but to that of other people—and for these sufferings they of course deserve compensation. If it is true to say that nothing that happens to us can be anything else than Karma—or the direct or indirect effect of a cause—it would be a great error to think that every evil or good which befalls us is due *only* to our own personal *Karma. (Vide* further on.)

[2] Our immortal and reincarnating principle in conjunction with the Manasic recollections of the preceding lives is called Sûtrâtmâ, which means literally the Thread-Soul; because like the pearls on a thread so is the long series of human lives strung together on that one thread. Manas must become *taijasi,* the radiant, before it can hang on the Sûtrâtma as a pearl on its thread, and so have full and absolute perception of itself in the Eternity. As said before, too close association with the terrestrial mind of the human soul alone causes this radiance to be entirely lost.

slightest recollection of a preceding life or any fact or event concerning it. . . . I may forget in the morning what I have dreamed during the night, still I know that I have slept and have the certainty that I lived during sleep; but what recollection have I of my past incarnation? How do you reconcile this?

M. Yet some people do recollect their past incarnations. This is what the Arhats call Samma-Sambuddha—or the knowledge of the whole series of one's past incarnations.

X. But we ordinary mortals who have not reached Samma-Sambuddha, how can we be expected to realize this simile?

M. By studying it and trying to understand more correctly the characteristics of the three states of sleep. Sleep is a general and immutable law for man as for beast, but there are different kinds of sleep and still more different dreams and visions.

X. Just so. But this takes us from our subject. Let us return to the materialist, who, while not denying dreams, which he could hardly do, yet denies immortality in general and the survival of his own individuality especially.

M. And the materialist is right for once, at least; since for one who has no inner perception and faith, there is no immortality possible. In order to live in the world to come a conscious life, one has to believe first of all in that life during one's terrestrial existence. On these two aphorisms of the Secret Science all the philosophy about the *post-mortem* consciousness and the immortality of the soul is built. The Ego receives always according to its deserts. After the dissolution of the body, there commences for it either a period of full clear consciousness, a state of chaotic dreams, or an utterly dreamless sleep indistinguishable from annihilation; and these are the three states of consciousness. Our physiologists find the cause of dreams and visions in an unconscious preparation for them during the waking hours; why cannot the same be admitted for the *post-mortem* dreams? I repeat it, *death is sleep.* After death begins, before the spiritual eyes of the soul, a performance according to a program learned and very often composed unconsciously by ourselves; the practical carrying out of *correct* beliefs or of illusions which have been created by ourselves. A Methodist will be a Methodist, a Mussulman a Mussulman, of course, just for a time—in a perfect fool's paradise of each man's creation and making. These are the *post-mortem* fruits of the tree of life. Naturally, our belief or unbelief in the fact of conscious immortality is unable to influence the unconditioned reality of the fact itself, once that it exists; but the belief or unbelief in that immortality, as the continuation or annihilation of separate entities, cannot fail to give color to that fact in its application to each of these entities. Now do you begin to understand it?

X. I think I do. The materialist, disbelieving in everything that cannot be proven to him by his five senses or by scientific reasoning, and rejecting every spiritual manifestation, accepts life as the only conscious existence. Therefore, according to their beliefs so will it be unto them. They will lose their personal Ego, and will plunge into a dreamless sleep until a new awakening. Is it so?

M. Almost so. Remember the universal esoteric teaching of the two kinds of conscious existence: the terrestrial and the spiritual. The latter must be considered real from the very fact that it is the region of the eternal, changeless, immortal cause of all; whereas the incarnating Ego dresses itself up in new garments entirely different from those of its previous incarnations, and in which all except its spiritual prototype is doomed to a change so radical as to leave no trace behind.

X. Stop! . . . Can the consciousness of my terrestrial *Egos* perish not only for a time, like the consciousness of the materialist, but in any case so entirely as to leave no trace behind?

M. According to the teaching, it must so perish and in its fulness, all except that principle which, having united itself with the Monad, has thereby become a purely spiritual and indestructible essence, one with it in the Eternity. But in the case of an out and out materialist, in whose personal "I" no Buddhi has ever reflected itself, how can the latter carry away into the infinitudes one particle of that terrestrial personality? Your spiritual "I" is immortal; but from your present Self it can carry away into after-life but that which has become worthy of immortality, namely, the aroma alone of the flower that has been mown by death.

X. Well, and the flower, the terrestrial "I"?

M. The flower, as all past and future flowers which blossomed and died, and will blossom again on the mother bough, the *Sûtrâtmâ,* all children of one root or Buddhi, will return to dust. Your present "I," as you yourself know, is not the body now sitting before me, nor yet is it what I would call Manas-Sûtrâtmâ—but Sûtrâtmâ-Buddhi.

X. But this does not explain to me at all, why you call life after death immortal, infinite, and real, and the terrestrial life a simple phantom or illusion; since even that *post-mortem* life has limits, however much wider they may be than those of terrestrial life.

M. No doubt. The spiritual Ego of man moves in Eternity like a pendulum between the hours of life and death. But if these hours marking the periods of terrestrial and spiritual life are limited in their duration, and if the very number of such stages in Eternity between sleep and awakening, illusion and reality, has its beginning and its end, on the other hand the spiritual "Pilgrim" is eternal. Therefore are the hours of his *post-mortem* life—when, disembodied he stands face to face with truth and not the mirages of his transitory earthly existences during the period of that pilgrimage which we call "the cycle of rebirths"—the only reality in our conception. Such intervals, their limitation notwithstanding, do not prevent the Ego, while ever perfecting itself, to be following undeviatingly, though gradually and slowly, the path to its last transformation, when that Ego having reached its goal becomes the divine ALL. These intervals and stages help towards this final result instead of hindering it; and without such limited intervals the divine Ego could never reach its ultimate goal. This Ego is the actor, and its numerous and various incarnations the parts it plays. Shall you call these parts with their costumes the individuality of the actor himself? Like that actor, the Ego is forced to play during the Cycle of Necessity up to the very threshold of *Paranirvâna* many parts such as may be unpleasant to it. But as the bee collects its honey from every flower, leaving the rest as food for the earthly worms, so does our spiritual individuality, whether we call it Sûtrâtmâ or Ego. It collects from every terrestrial personality into which Karma forces it to incarnate, the nectar alone of the spiritual qualities and self-consciousness, and uniting all these into one whole it emerges from its chrysalis as the glorified Dhyâni Chohan. So much the worse for those terrestrial personalities from which it could collect nothing. Such personalities cannot assuredly outlive consciously their terrestrial existence.

X. Thus then it seems, that for the terrestrial personality, immortality is still conditional. Is then immortality itself *not* unconditional?

M. Not at all. But it cannot touch the *non-existent*. For all that which exists as SAT, ever aspiring to SAT, immortality and Eternity are absolute. Matter is the opposite pole of spirit and yet the two are one. The essence of all this, *i. e.*, Spirit, Force and Matter, or the three in one, is as endless as it is beginningless; but the form acquired by the triple unity during incarnations, the externality, is certainly only the illusion of our personal conceptions. Therefore do we call the after-life alone a reality, while relegating the terrestrial life, its terrestrial personality included, to the phantom realm of illusion.

X. But why in such a case not call sleep the reality, and waking the illusion, instead of the reverse?

M. Because we use an expression made to facilitate the grasping of the subject, and from the standpoint of terrestrial conceptions, it is a very correct one.

X. Nevertheless, I cannot understand. If the life to come is based on justice and the merited retribution for all our terrestrial suffering, how, in the case of materialists many of whom are ideally honest and charitable men, should there remain of their personality nothing but the refuse of a faded flower!

M. No one ever said such a thing. No materialist, if a good man, however unbelieving, can die forever in the fulness of his spiritual individuality. What was said is, that the consciousness of one life can disappear either fully or partially; in the case of a thorough materialist, no vestige of that personality which disbelieved remains in the series of lives.

X. But is this not annihilation to the Ego?

M. Certainly not. One can sleep a dead sleep during a long railway journey, miss one or several stations without the slightest recollection or consciousness of it, awake at another station and continue the journey recollecting other halting places, till the end of that journey, when the goal is reached. Three kinds of sleep were mentioned to you: the dreamless, the chaotic, and the one so real, that to the sleeping man his dreams become full realities. If you believe in the latter why can't you believe in the former? According to what one has believed in and expected after death, such is the state one will have. He who expected no life to come will have an absolute blank amounting to annihilation in the interval between the two rebirths. This is just the carrying out of the program we spoke of, and which is created by the materialist himself. But there are various kinds of materialists, as you say. A selfish wicked Egoist, one who never shed a tear for anyone but himself, thus adding entire indifference to the whole world to his unbelief, must drop at the threshold of death his personality for ever. This personality having no tendrils of sympathy for the world around, and hence nothing to hook on to the string of the Sûtrâtmâ, every connection between the two is broken with the last breath. There being no Devachan for such a materialist, the Sûtrâtmâ will re-incarnate almost immediately. But those materialists who erred in nothing but their disbelief, will oversleep but one station. Moreover, the time will come when the ex-materialist will perceive himself in the Eternity and perhaps repent that he lost even one day, or station, from the life eternal.

X. Still, would it not be more correct to say that death is birth into a new life, or a return once more to the threshold of eternity?

M. You may if you like. Only remember that births differ, and that there are births of "still-born" beings, which are failures. Moreover, with your fixed Western ideas about material life, the words "living" and "being" are quite inapplicable to the pure subjective state of *post-mortem* existence. It is just because of such ideas—save in a few philosophers who are not read by the many and who themselves are too confused to present a distinct picture of it—that all your conceptions of life and death have finally become so narrow. On the one hand, they have led to crass materialism, and on the other, to the still more material conception of the other life which the Spiritualists have formulated in their Summer-land. There the souls of men eat, drink, and marry, and live in a Paradise quite as sensual as that of Mohammed, but even less philosophical. Nor are the average conceptions of the uneducated Christians any better, but are still more material, if possible. What between truncated Angels, brass trumpets, golden harps, streets in paradisiacal cities paved with jewels, and hell-fires, it seems like a scene at a Christmas pantomime. It is because of these narrow conceptions that you find such difficulty in understanding. And, it is also just because the life of the disembodied soul, while possessing all the vividness of reality, as in certain dreams, is devoid of every grossly objective form of terrestrial life, that the Eastern philosophers have compared it with visions during sleep.

Made in the USA
Monee, IL
27 February 2020